Twer Levels of Self- Deception

REVISED EDITION
by
Tom Wallace

Other books by Tom Wallace:

Conatus

Three Miles of Rice Pudding

Utopia Governance and the Commons

A Little Book About Climate Change

Vocatus atque, non vocatus deus arderit.

('Summoned or not, a god will be present.'
Written on the lintel of the house of Carl Jung)

TWENTY-ONE LEVELS OF SELF-DECEPTION

Table of Contents

PREFACE TO THE REVISED EDITION   7

INTRODUCTION   9

PART 1 – EROS   13

1. ALL IS ONE   13
2. SOMETHING AND NOTHING   25
3. PHENOMENA AND THE NOUMENON   35
4. MIND IS SPLIT   41
5. ASCENDANCY AND DESCENDANCY   47
6. ASCENDANCY IS SPIRIT   51
7. DESCENDANCY IS SOUL   57
8. ASCENDANCY DOMINATES   65

PART 2 - AGAPÉ   73

9. THE WORLD IS DISENCHANTED   73
11. DESIRE IS ALWAYS AMBIGUOUS   85
12. MEANING WILL ALWAYS ALLUDE US   91
13. THE SOUL SEEKS BEAUTY FIRST   99
14. START WITH AWE   109
15. CELEBRATE LIFE   113
16. ALLOW FOR DARKNESS, CHAOS AND
RANDOMNESS   121
17. BEWARE IDEALS   127
18. INTRINSIC VALUE   131
19. DERIVE ETHICS FROM RELATIONSHIPS   135

20. COMPASSION AND DESIRE MEET IN EMBODIED PERSONS   **141**

21. BE THE MEANS OF GRACE   **149**

CONCLUSION   **159**

Preface to the Revised Edition

This revised edition contains only minor edits from the original. Kindle editions have been re-formatted to be the same page size as the paperback edition.

I regard this book as a 'commons' and am happy for it to be shared, in any format, on any platform, provided that an acknowledgement is given to the author and links provided back to where I have posted the manuscript.

TWENTY-ONE LEVELS OF SELF-DECEPTION

Introduction

'The world being illusive, one must be deluded in some way if one is to triumph in it.'

W.B. Yeats

Each chapter of this work is presented as a delusion. As Chapter 1 indicates, the fundamental delusion is to think that we can say anything at all about the nature of reality. Realty is an experience beyond words or logical analysis. The chances of getting anywhere near truth are therefore negligible! Reading however is an interruption to the flow of life and sometimes a word or phrase can resonate with an individual and provide some small help. That is the hope and intention here. There are also 'mustard seed moments', when the mind is open to new truth and some small word or thought arrives just at that time.

If truth is unknowable or inexpressible, then at least there is truth within a particular context — so far as we are able to realise this. I draw back from describing this as relative truth. The way I describe it is to recognise that when we are discussing a particular matter we do this within a context or boundary, whether this is recognised or not. Some boundaries are constructions that we make for ourselves. Some boundaries are forced upon us. Some boundaries are present but are not acknowledged or are misunderstood or denied. Only in the broadest context of Chapter 1, All is One, is there no boundary by definition. All other discussions are made therefore in opposition (but not in conflict) to this stance.

In like manner, some chapters speak of 'economies' and I use this word to define a bounded set of transactions, such as the 'economy of grace'. Where such terms are employed it is again to try to sharpen our understanding of what is at stake when we use language and make assumptions unconsciously. Looking at the world in terms of distinct economies often serves as a useful tool to highlight points of contention or agreement that otherwise may be overlooked.

I make the distinction between Eros and Agapé but it is a difficult one. Eros should be spoken of mainly in positive terms, but the 'ascendant' aspect of Eros — always seeking higher and further goals — has to a large extent eclipsed the 'descendant' aspect. (Ascendancy and descendancy are terms we will be looking at in some detail within the work.) I have identified this ascendancy primarily with 'spirit'. I do not use the word to imply any pre-existing entity who inhabits us, or some aspect of ourselves that might survive bodily death. Rather it is to try to emphasise the rarefied, aspirational aspect that is so much part of western religion, science and culture. Likewise, I use the word 'soul' to designate all that is 'descendant' in human nature and not in any sense to suggest that the soul can have a separate existence. 'Descendant' is used by way of contrast to 'ascendant'. However, the notion of going 'down' and embracing the Earth and other people is perhaps somewhat difficult. In a way we are already 'down' — or more properly we are in the midst, surrounded, enfolded, embraced and cherished by nature. However, as we so often assume the hierarchical role of ascendancy, then we need some going down just to bring us back to where we really are. We need to acknowledge our true relation with nature and culture. In contrast to Eros, Agapé is probably closer to the descendant aspect of life.

Where to begin then, in trying to explain what the aim of this book is about? Well, two things:

I want to celebrate life — my body, my relationship with other people, my place in nature and my place within the wider universe. This is the erotic nature of life seeking expression. But various things seem to prevent me from fully realising this goal. How can this be resolved? Added to this, I see the suffering of others. I want to help meet their needs. Again though, this desire is frustrated. My own search for happiness and the suffering of others are difficult problems to relieve. What can be done to remedy this?

In essence, these two questions are the premise of the work. Personal happiness — explored best perhaps in psychoanalysis — and happiness for the many, the Marxist ideology. Desire and need.

Psychoanalysis literally means 'letting the butterfly go free.' And Freud spoke of the 'will to pleasure'. Meanwhile the frustration of this quest is succinctly observed by R.D. Laing in *The Politics of Experience and the Bird of Paradise*. He says: 'To adapt to this world, the child abdicates its ecstasy.' Recovering ecstasy then is the first quest of this work.

As for the second issue — satisfying the needs of others — we have to face the fact that the political solution has not been ultimately realisable and address our concerns accordingly.

Our culture tends to see questions as either/or questions. It tries to reduce everything in the world to such black and white choices. The alternative to this dualistic, polemical approach is a 'dialectic' − a discussion that looks at both/and. I hope that what follows will be such a dialectic. Always, the 'delusions' we discuss are not to be abandoned wholesale. Of particular note is how we might 'bring home' each subject to real life and how it might inform us of our response to ourselves, others and to the world.

Finally, of course, I am not pretending to 'solve' the delusions discussed here. They are probably unsolvable. If you are looking for answers then stop reading now! If however, you are content with 'going nowhere in a timeless moment' then read on!

Part 1 – Eros

1. All is One

*'Before the world was
And the sky was filled with stars...
There was a strange unfathomable Body.
This being, this Body is silent
And beyond substance and sensing.
It stretches beyond everything spanning the empyrean.
It has always been here and it always will be.
Everything comes from it, and then it is the Mother of Everything.
I do not know its name. So I call it TAO.'*

In the classic Seventies book *Zen and the Art of Motorcycle Maintenance*, Robert Pirsig said that a lot can be learnt from where people choose to make the first 'split' in the world. Religion for instance might take the split to be between light and darkness, or perhaps heaven and Earth. In philosophy and in science the most obvious split is between 'subjects' and 'objects'.

Our increasingly science-based, technology-driven, industrialised culture recognises only objects in its world view and discounts the reality of subjective experience. Hence, morals and aesthetics, both considered subjective, are given less and less prominence. There is no *'quality'* recognised as real, only *'quantity'*. Hence, the *'Disqualified Universe'* (Max Weber). In *Zen and the Art of Motorcycle Maintenance* Pirsig essentially sets out a metaphysics of quality. The book is subtitled *An Enquiry into Values* — it puts quality in the place of truth as the ultimate reality. We will return to this idea in a later chapter, but for now let's look at what it means for there to be a split in the world.

David Bohm, in his book *Wholeness and the Implicate Order* looks at the sentence, 'It is raining'. What, he asks, is the 'it' that is doing the raining? Why do we not just say: 'Rain is going on'? Clearly, language has created a subject and an object, even where there is not strictly speaking the need to make such a distinction. The point is to illustrate how deeply embedded in our culture and thinking such splits in the world really are. Even language is framed to assume such divisions in the world, so we often adopt them unconsciously and simply as a part of growing up and learning our mother tongue.

Ourselves and others, theism and atheism, future and past, transcendence and immanence — all of these are further splits embedded in our culture. So too is the manner in which words are regarded either as simple signifiers or set within a context. Transcendence and imminence is a further polarity that has a particular bearing on the development of the argument within this work. We will consider each of these dualities below. Two really big splits take a bit more investigation: the difference between something and nothing and what we might call our innate ideas about the world contrasted with our actual experience. From Kant, and other philosophers, I use the terms noumenon and phenomenon for this split. The split between something and nothing will form the basis of Chapter 2, whilst the noumenon phenomenon division of reality is the subject of Chapter 3. I have of course introduced deliberately two other major splits — that between Eros and Agapé and that between ascendancy and descendancy. The manner in which these terms are employed in this work is discussed in the Introduction. The reader is reminded that I do not regard any of these splits as real. I am employing them with the deliberate intent of drawing out an understanding of the issues raised within the text. I am also looking to challenge those splits which explicitly or implicitly are embedded in our culture and to see how this has often been a cause of harm.

To some extent, we have been forced into these kinds of dualisms simply in order to survive in the world. We make a distinction first of all about ourselves as subjects, distinct from the world around us. In other words, we 'objectify' the world, including, to some extent, other people. Science merely formalises this notion of the 'detached observer', which is implicit in so much of our language and thinking — whilst philosophy describes this as 'the view from nowhere' (Thomas Nagel). It is a remarkably successful strategy for surviving in the world, but we have come to believe of course that this split is real – that consciousness and matter really are separate substances. Much of western philosophy has been about trying to reconcile the two apparently distinct substances and has tied itself in knots in the process. This is the so-called 'mind body problem' — *res cogita, res extensa* — most usually associated with Descartes.

The subject object split, as was said, leads us into 'objectifying' others — treating them to an extent as commodities rather than as individual persons. We will be examining this in more detail throughout the work. Also, there has been an assumption that considering ourselves as subjects is just a simple notion. Psychoanalysis has shown however that becoming a subject is actually a very fraught process, involving by definition, the suppression of desire. (The denial of Eros — hence very pertinent to our discussion.) It is also a process that as currently described, is deeply related to death and is heavily misogynistic, both in its conception and in its consequences. Again, this will be considered more in later chapters.

In the theism-atheism duality, the question: 'Is there a God?' is too simplistic. The kind of separate, fully transcendent being that is normally implied by the question can be seen as just another way in which we choose to split reality. The distinction then between 'God' and 'not God' and so between 'believer' and 'unbeliever' is arbitrary. In fact, the way this polarity is contested simply reinforces the underlying assumptions on which both theism and atheism are built. The God who is rejected by atheists is the same God who is embraced (or feared) by believers. The understanding of what or who 'God' might be is never really contested. We may contrast this with the kind of Pantheism advocated by Spinoza, in which there is only one substance, which is God, and mind and matter are seen as twin attributes of this single underlying reality. Alternative ways of viewing all dualities are clearly possible, and the theism atheism duality illustrates this particularly well because the two 'sides' of the duality are so fiercely contested.

Past, present and future are likewise just convenient ways of carving up reality. In a sense, time does not exist. We divide ourselves up by thinking about what we would like to be in the future, or things that we would like to achieve. Again, whilst this is helpful in terms of making plans, it is actually a false split. There is no future me, or past me. We are all that we ever will be just in this moment! So, regretting the past or worrying over the future are pointless abstractions. Planning for the future in a reasonable manner however is to make proper use of this artificial split in the world.

There is also a split in the world with any kind of description — in fact any word causes such a split. As soon as we use a word to describe something, we automatically assign all other things as being something else. Hence, calling something a table immediately creates a split between things that belong to the description as tables and things that don't. However, this is no more than just a convenient way to carve up the world. Many things could serve as 'tables' for instance, so the description is not really an accurate one — it is just a useful designation that fits our purposes. In fact it is a little more difficult than this. To describe something as a 'table' is to use a word as a simple signifier and it might be assumed that all words, if used clearly enough and with correct construction of sentences, would act in the same way (much in the manner of Bertrand Russell attempting to formulate logic by means of language). Context however creates a worldview in which individual words sit. As such, the meaning of individual words is at least partly dependant on context and an individual's familiarity or otherwise with that context. A worldview — perhaps all world views — are therefore 'constructed'. In this work, the context of our discussion is given by defining boundaries and 'economies'.

In a similar vein, we distinguish between 'transcendent' ideals such as truth, goodness and beauty and their representations (or immanence) in the world. Values then come to be seen as having some kind of ghostly existence of their own — even sometimes for people who have no religious belief. The Platonic forms — perhaps the most familiar example of transcendent ideals — are now widely rejected, but covertly still applied. Consider for instance the writings of physicists about mathematical truths. Scientism thus has an insidious grip — science claims to speak from a position of neutrality, but in fact has underlying assumptions that go unchallenged. There is for instance an underlying desire in science (and western culture generally) that is denied — perhaps we could call it power over nature. This in turn is derived from the culture's repressed obsession with death that expresses itself as 'power over' and 'power under' dynamics (sadomasochism). Western politics has followed suit. Religion, at least in the west, actually reinforces this approach rather than contesting it. There is a reaching for an objective 'hook' on which to hang subjective notions of spirituality. Perhaps we want to believe in some kind of real 'transcendence', something more than just transcendence of value, as spoken of above. In doing so, we may fail to see that this is just one more way of conveniently carving up reality. Jean Paul Sartre describes people like this as 'the serious' — that is, they take seriously the reality of transcendent values. A constant theme of this work is the tendency to try to make so many things transcendent. We will return to this several times as the argument progresses and seek to rediscover the immanence of value that has been marginalised or overlooked.

There is a quality of discernment that we can bring to questions and situations that respects all of the notions mentioned above. Perhaps the best way to describe it is to contrast dualist or polemic with dialectic. Or, to put it more simply — 'both /and' rather than 'either/or'. A restriction of knowledge is recognised and the two oppositions are weighed against one another. The result is not necessarily a mixture of both sides, nor necessarily a 'third way', as both these options suggest some kind of final outcome. The discernment is instead a 'conversation' between the various options — and this conversation may continue indefinitely.

We turn now however to consider the essential oneness of reality. Of course, even saying that ultimate reality is one thing falls foul of the same problems described above. Jonathan Culler writes about the problem of describing reality in these terms:

'We are on dangerous ground even with such "innocent" phrases as "All is One". The Universe is not a whole, nor a collection of parts, but a "holarchy". An ever-receding domain of wholes within parts within wholes. There is no boundary either "upwards" (to larger groupings of parts) or "downwards" (to increasing fine divisions of wholes).

'Total context (final Wholeness) is unmasterable, both in principle and in practice. *Meaning is context bound, but context is boundless*'

Ken Wilber, in commenting on this passage, says this:

'The mind's omega point, for each theorist, is the context that they believe cannot be outcontexted, the context beyond which growth or expansion does not or should not proceed...

'And a final Omega Point? That would imply a final Whole, and there is no such holon anywhere in manifest existence. But perhaps we can interpret it differently. Who knows, perhaps Telos, perhaps Eros, moves the entire Kosmos, and God may indeed be an all-embracing chaotic Attractor, acting...throughout the world by gentle persuasion toward love.'

Ken Wilber — Sex, *Ecology, Spirituality*

Again, our boundaries and economies are the means deployed in this work of setting contexts and therefore recognising parochial meaning. Such discussions therefore often use the term 'nondual', meaning simply, 'not two'. This is really the closest that we can come in words to describing the indescribable. (Indeed, Wilber is one of the chief contemporary proponents of nonduality.)

Nonduality might seem at first a subject rather distant from our concerns of the self's search for satisfaction of desire and meeting the needs of others. However, Jerry Katz, in his book *Essential Writings on Nonduality*, speaks about desire and the self being entwined:

'Our heart's desire and who, what and where we are, are not separate.
'Our pursuit for truth is for the full recognition of non-separation, not-two-ness, or nonduality. The value of this quality of desire is confirmed in the first verse of the scripture from Hindu tradition known as the Avadhuta Ghita, or Song of the Free:
"Through the grace of God alone, the desire for nonduality arises in wise people to save them from fear."
'The need for knowing nonduality, or non-separation from truth, is grace, a profound gift arising from truth. The desire, the Avadhuta Ghita says, arises in wise people. We could say the hunger for nonduality is wisdom. Wisdom is allowing the desire for nonduality to unfold. That is the way to be saved from fear.'

> Jerry Katz — *Essential Writings on Nonduality*

Katz goes on to explain the nature of the fear that nonduality saves us from. One fear is simply our own non-existence in death, the other fear is that we may be spending our lives desiring the wrong things. We will return to these ideas later in the work.

21

Desire is usually seen as an endless process of searching. It was Hegel who suggested that this process could only be brought to a satisfactory conclusion in belief. The nature of Western religion, philosophy and science in particular have frustrated this aim by making 'God' into an object, creating an image of a transcendent fulfilled (that is, desire-satisfying) life beyond this one and reinforcing rather than solving the desire that is manifest in all of us. The satisfaction of desire by means of transcendent belief is a notion that needs to be challenged, and this will occupy us in later chapters.

There is no striving for nonduality — it is just recognised or it is not. Nonduality is just ordinary life; it's not enlightenment, or nirvana or samadhi necessarily, although of course it contains all of these. So there is nothing to do, except to give up our search, to deny the ever-receding horizon of desire that is our inheritance as divided 'subjects' in the world. Or if you are not searching, then don't begin. Either way, we have all already arrived.

Katz goes on to explain that even describing this view as a 'nondual perspective' is itself contradictory:

'The nondual perspective, because it is a perspective, a view of something, is dualistic. By considering the oxymoron "nondual perspective", we get a better sense of how things remain distinct whilst being non-separate.'
>   Jerry Katz — *Essential Writings on Nonduality*

Perhaps we can just say, when I fully surrender to the moment, I am that moment — completely present. The 'not-two' or nonduality of reality is therefore central to this work. Already, the element of Eros is present — the hunger for desire to be satisfied, and a clue to the satisfaction of that hunger by the bringing together of self and nonduality. We will look at two further divisions in our view of reality — something and nothing, and phenomena and the noumenon — prior to developing the argument further.

TWENTY-ONE LEVELS OF SELF-DECEPTION

2. Something and Nothing

'Nothing. Nothing is an awe-inspiring yet essentially undigested concept, highly esteemed by writers of a mystical or existential tendency, but by most others regarded with anxiety, nausea, or panic.'

Encyclopaedia of Philosophy

Truth has taken on a special pre-eminence in modern times. Despite the onslaught of post-modernism, somehow, there is an inherent belief in an absolute truth in the form of verifiable correspondence with the observable world as being at least theoretically possible. The notion still holds sway even although looking more closely at such truth claims leads inevitably to an ever-receding horizon of possible knowledge about the world. Look close enough at matter, or energy, or force and they simply evaporate. Is there anything absolutely true? Perhaps just the statement 'something is going on'! But even that might be up for question. Even the difference between something and nothing might not ultimately be real.

The entire world is like this! When one looks closely at words and descriptions and questions, they carve up the world in the manner described above. Very big questions therefore are suspect. They are asked with the assumption that there could be a clear meaning to the question and a straightforward answer that we could understand. But unfortunately the world is not like this. The way language splits the world is a false split, as previously described. There can only be one universe — by definition — and therefore even at this level, any divisions in the universe are just our descriptions – our way of seeing the world.

There is one really fundamental question and that is:- 'Why is there something rather than nothing?' (It was apparently Leibniz who first raised this as a philosophical concern – there has to be a 'sufficient reason' for something to be.) Is this question at least immune from the concerns raised above? I would have to say, no, it's not! Even the difference between something and nothing is a false split.

Buddhism has a way of speaking about ultimate reality, in that all statements must be qualified by three others. So if we say: 'the universe exists', we make a split in the universe by suggesting that all non-existent things do not belong to it. Hence, we need to qualify our statement by also saying: 'the universe does not exist" 'the universe both exists and does not exist,' and finally, 'the universe neither exists nor does it not exist.' Clearly, even all four statements about the universe taken together don't really tell us anything. And that of course is the whole point — no statement about ultimate reality really makes any sense. It is only by defining boundaries, and assuming parochial economies of human endeavour or ecology or whatever that we can get to a place where statements can take on a meaning. Our statements and questions will then be qualified by the limits that we knowingly impose upon ourselves.

What then of something and nothing? It is more than simply a matter of saying there could have been nothing, but instead there's something or saying something and nothing are the same. It might seem like a very strange point to make, but our culture has an inherent bias towards something. Nothing is regarded as an absence – almost a mistake. Our view of reality might be very different indeed if we were to turn this on its head and see something arising out of nothing. Consider this explanation of the issue given by Wu Wei Wei, commenting on the Diamond Sutra and quoted by Jerry Katz:

'The importance of this understanding of the precedence of the negative element to the positive, of the void to the plenum, of non-being to being, of I am not to I am is sufficiently great to justify any degree of hyperbole — for it requires a reversal of our habitual way of regarding these matters, and a transvaluation of our established values according to which...we assume positive reality or being and then look for negatives. That is, we imagine the void as an emptiness in a pre-existing fullness, a nothing in an assumed something, whereas we are urgently required to apprehend the ubiquitous pre-existence of nothing, out of which something may appear, or out of non-manifestation manifestation.'

So, whilst in one sense — regarding all as one — we are obliged to regard something and nothing as a false split; nonetheless, when we look closer at this duality, the usual manner of understanding is perhaps flawed. We assume nothing to be almost a product of something or at least the absence of something rather than giving nothing its true and balanced weight.

Again, it may seem like a subtle point, but so much of what we do gives pre-eminence to existence. Even for instance St. Anslem's famous proof for the existence of God uses the precedence of existence over non-existence as a reason for belief. The whole basis of empirical science — that is, science based on observation — makes the underlying assumption that existence is primary and that extension in space and time are basic to that existence. Logical positivism extended this notion to effectively dismiss the unseen as irrelevant and unreal. Science has so far made an exception for forces — gravity, electro-magnetism and the strong and weak nuclear force — but the search always seems to be on to find particles which facilitate these forces — to render them material. Subjectivity and with it emotion, spirituality, desire and passion, have often therefore been rendered non-existent. We will see in later chapters the immense damage this has done, not least to women and to the feminine aspect of reality. However, we will also see how non-material things — in the pursuit of ideals – have been covertly rendered into qualities of being. For instance, happiness has become something that we might possess or earn, as if it were a physical thing. Ethics changed to metaphysics, in the relentless materialisation of the world.

In Greek mythology, first there was chaos and then one of the earliest gods to be born was Eros. Eros is able to bring order out of chaos. Eros is the creative attraction of opposites and the order that can result. To be erotic is to love and affirm life! This brings us to another aspect of the something and nothing question, the contrast between creation from nothing (`ex nihilo´) as opposed to order out of chaos. If we were to adopt order out of chaos we might also say becoming rather than beginning.

Chaos creates the couple Erebos (darkness) and Nyx (night) who in turn birthed Hypnos, the god of sleep. Together with Pasithea, goddess of relaxation and hallucination, Hypnos fathered the three lords of the dream kingdom — Morpheus, Phobetor and Phantasos, who ruled over the changeable, fearful and fantastical regions of life. Hypnosis' court is guarded by Aergia — literally, inactivity — goddess of sloth. From this we can note that chaos (rather than just `nothingness´) is always attempting to gain a foothold in human life. We need to be doing a bit of work to keep order in place and chaos at bay.

Grace Jantzen, who we will hear more from in later chapters, contrasts the usual word for a person — `mortal´ — with `natal´. In suggesting this name, she is asking us to consider: Are we beginning just to die or are we born in order to become?

Theologian Catherine Keller has written extensively over this contrast of something out of nothing and order out of chaos. She says:

'Beginning is going on. Everywhere. Amidst all the endings, so rarely ripe or ready. They show up late, these beginnings, bristling with promise, yet laboured and doomed. Every last one of them is lovingly addressed "in the beginning". But if such talk-talk of the beginning at the end has produced the poles, the boundary markers of a closed totality, if "the beginning" has blocked the disruptive infinities of becoming, then theology had better get out of its own way.'

Catherine Keller — *Face of the Deep* — *A Theology of Becoming*.

Keller goes on to talk of becoming as a process emerging from chaos:

'If we discern a third space of beginning – neither pure origin nor nihilist flux – its difference translates into another interstitial space; that between the self-presence of a changeless being who somehow suddenly (back then) created; and the pure nonbeing out of which that creation was summoned, and towards which its fluency falls. That alternative milieu, neither being nor nonbeing, will signify the site of becoming as *genesis*; the topos of the Deep. Can we tell the story this way; that *tehom* (the deep) as primal chaos precedes and gives rise to the generative tensions of order and disorder, form and formlessness? Might *tehom* henceforth suggest the chaoid (so not necessarily chaotic) multidimensionality of a bottomless Deep; the matrix in which the creation *becomes*? In which the strange inter-fluences of creatures — in ecology, predation, cultures — crisscross the abyss of difference?

> Catherine Keller — *Face of the Deep — A Theology of Becoming*.

In similar vein, the Buddhist tradition recognises the concept of 'Sunyata'. It is described thus:

'To call it being is wrong, because only concrete things exist. To call it non-being is wrong. It is best to avoid all description.... It is the basis of all. The absolute, the truth that cannot be preached in words.'

> Heinrich Zimmer — *Philosophies of India*.

Generally speaking, science favours creation '*ex nihilo*'. If some previously-existing chaotic state were envisaged, then science presumably would feel the need to explain this somehow. In balance, although creation out of a literal nothing is not an entirely satisfactory explanation, it is probably preferable and less messy for science than order out of chaos. On the basis of Occam's Razor — science inevitably opts for this simpler answer. Already, on a small scale, such 'creation' is accepted, as when two mutually opposing particles 'appear' and then almost instantaneously annihilate each other.

A beginning, as mentioned by Catherine Keller, implies an end. The universe does not simply risk sliding back into chaos, it faces total extinction. Again, there is an underlying association with death in the choice of viewing the creation in this way.

The acceptance of this notion of a literal nothingness from which the universe sprung also ties in with the notion that we are here by chance. However, life defies the second law of thermodynamics — it effectively makes order where chaos should rein. Therefore, science's preference for creation out of nothing implicitly suggests that life is an anomaly. The way things stand there is a covert interest in dead matter over an interest in life and this awkward bias is studiously ignored. If we were instead to opt for order out of chaos from the outset then life would be seen to be contiguous with the birth and development of the universe.

As Catherine Keller has indicated, form and formlessness are better terms to describe creation than something and nothing. The flux between form and formlessness is an important aspect of life, to which we will return. In the meantime, we can relate these ideas back to what was said about nonduality in Chapter 1. According to Ngakpa Chogyam, nonduality has two sides:

'One is the empty, or nonduality, and the other is form or duality. Therefore, duality is not illusory but is instead one *aspect* of nonduality. Like the two sides of a coin, the formless reality has two dimensions — one is form, the other is formless. When we perceive duality as separate from nonduality (or nonduality as separate from duality) we do not engage with the world of manifestation from a perspective of oneness, and thereby we fall into an erroneous relationship with it. From this perspective, it is not "life" or duality that is Maya or illusion; rather it is our relationship to the world that is

32

illusory.'

> Ngakpa Chogyam
> (As quoted by Mariana Caplan in *Eyes Wide Open; Cultivating Discernment on the Spiritual Path.*)

A literal nothing is very difficult to conceive. When the term is used in common parlance it is in a more circumscribed manner. For instance, we may speak of 'empty' space, a cloudless sky or a street devoid of people or cars. In so doing, we realise of course that this is not a literal nothing. However, that emptiness or vacancy of which we speak has a lot more to say to us than an inaccessible and literal nothingness. It is the spaces between thoughts and words. The small silences in a piece of music. The time of rest between work or action in the world. The time spent alone in between time spent with family, friends or colleagues. The time spent just doing 'nothing'. It seems to me that these are all necessary counterpoints to the 'somethings' that we are busily seeking or creating in the world. Letting go of 'somethings' allows a space from which new ideas and new forms can be created. Letting go will be a theme to which we will return.

Formlessness then is far from being empty — in fact formlessness is ever ripe with potential. We make the mistake of seeing 'nothingness' as a negative — an absence of stuff — rather than as a potential for birth and the underlying essence of all that is. Order out of chaos, form out of formlessness.

3. Phenomena and the Noumenon

'That of which we cannot speak, we must pass over in silence.'

Ludwig Wittgenstein — Tractatus Logico-Philosophicus

The '...very being of anything, whereby it is what it is. And thus, the real internal, but generally unknown constitution of things, wherein their discoverable qualities depend, may be called their essence.'

John Locke

The noumenon was originally noumena — plural — contrasting with phenomena. Phenomena are just things that can be experienced and measured, whilst noumena are either hidden things or the hidden aspect of a phenomenon. This is all from Kant. Noumena were perhaps not therefore originally meant to be that mysterious. It is just that as humans we are limited to three dimensions of space and one of time and so are inevitably limited in what we can actually either directly experience or measure. Because things can be conceived without apparently any prior knowledge or perception on which the conception can be based, there must, Kant argued be an underlying reality to allow this conception to occur. Since Kant's time of course we have discovered that there may be extra dimensions of space that we are unable to experience but can model with mathematics. It is not clear whether such spatial dimensions would still be noumena to Kant or have now become phenomena. Indeed, we might question whether space and time are quite as 'given' as Kant and science have assumed.

A more modern take is from physicist David Bohm. His *Wholeness and the Implicate Order* suggests a universe where physical things — and perhaps also consciousness — are rolled up, as it were and are 'implicate' in reality until they are experienced, or thought. Then they are 'explicated'. There is then an 'unfolding' which makes things and ideas 'explicate'.

It was the post-Kantian philosophers, Schelling, Hegel and Schopenhauer, who took the idea of noumena and phenomena forward from Kant's original version, and Schopenhauer in particular who made it noumenon, singular, and related it to the 'nondual' belief of Eastern religion. His main work, the title of which is usually translated from the German as *The World as Will and Representation*, is one of the key works of philosophy. The 'will' in the title is the noumenon and the 'representation' is the world of phenomena. Schopenhauer also introduced the idea of 'first person privilege' in that we can know our own thoughts in a way that no-one else can. He thought that the will was the hidden motivator behind our actions, primarily as the will to live.

Schopenhauer's ideas spawned a whole lot of post-modern thought including Nietzsche's will to power and Freud's will to pleasure. To Hegel, self-consciousness is desire.

Given what was said above about the noumenon perhaps originally not being intended to be 'mysterious' and also the possibility that what constitutes the noumenon may be eroded by new knowledge, I want to distinguish it in this work from what I will refer to as mystery. The noumenon may simply be what cannot be directly measured, and there is mystery beyond this — in fact an infinite regress of mystery such that we will never reach total understanding. For consistency with writers quoted later in this work, we could say that the essence of an individual emanates from mystery. To an extent similar to Schopenhauer's view that will emanates from the noumenon. Mystery is also the source of value. Robert Pirsig, in his book 'Zen and the Art of Motorcycle Maintenance' would have ultimate reality as 'dynamic quality' and then split up the phenomenal world in terms of static 'quality'. Value is therefore built into the universe by definition — in fact value defines the universe. Pirsig's account is very useful in illuminating just what we do and what we assume when we split the world into subject and object rather than aspects of value. Pirsig draws attention to the essential place of desire in all of life and shows how choosing and preferring are actually more fundamental to the way life is lived than rationality and intellect. These statements are provisional of course and as explained in the Introduction I do not intend such definitions to be taken literally. They are just convenient ways of viewing reality to see how our views of things may change if a different system is adopted. How different the world might look for instance if we believed that our essential nature, our essence or soul stands somehow outside of our everyday selves. Compare this with the idea that we are just the product of genetic information provided by our parents, perhaps with some random differences that cannot be accounted for. Both views are an act of faith really, and it is only our culture's bias towards a scientific world view that might make us favour the materialist version over the more mystical one.

We saw in an earlier chapter how regarding 'God' as an 'object' (that is, a fully transcendent ideal) brings difficulties. But to regard God as a subject also leads to problems. It leads to the very difficult questions that so-called 'unbelievers' often pose of religion. For instance, why does a good God allow evil to exist? In trying to make God into a person or at least somehow knowable, religion has actually made a belief that is as fallible as human reasoning. Could we equate God with the noumenon? That seems a troublesome possibility. (The 'will' for Schopenhauer, is something of a blind force.) It would be better to say that God is simply mystery and leave it at that. Perhaps Buddhism comes closest to this position. The Buddhist koans are designed to frustrate the normal linear human thinking in approaching ideas about ultimate reality. The most famous koan of course is: 'What is the sound of one hand clapping?'

Traditionally science has regarded everything to

be knowable and understandable, at least in theory, so it does not generally does not acknowledge the phenomenon/noumenon split. If any kind of unknown is acknowledged, it is simply as a result of lack of information. It is there, waiting for an explanation.

Science does not really believe in subjects — they are always regarded as derivatives of objects. Thus consciousness is merely a by-product of activities within the brain, which in turn are derived from objects. This has led to subjectivity being derided in our culture generally and thereby relegating questions of value and morality to ones of personal preference.

The phenomenon-noumenon split, like all our dualities, is something of a two-edged sword. On the one hand, it might suggest that attempts to comprehend the world will inevitably be thwarted. The noumenon, being fundamentally mysterious, will throw a spanner in the works as it were and make the operations of nature always incomprehensible. On the other hand, if the phenomenal world is the world as it appears through human understanding and via the constraints of the human senses then perhaps a complete and logically-consistent explanation of phenomena is achievable without interference from the mysterious noumenon. The noumenon is always there, but just as a ghost. On this view, for the purposes of human knowledge and understanding, it need not trouble us.

So, we have mystery, and indeed physicist John Wheeler has said that as the island of knowledge grows bigger, the shoreline onto the sea of mystery increases exponentially. Perhaps we are better to start by embracing the mystery rather than trying to deny it. That means to act from the assumption of ignorance rather than the assumption of knowledge. We might say that this is the response mystery calls from us concerning questions of truth or knowledge. Beauty and goodness — the other broad categories of value — also emanate from mystery. Bertrand Russell for instance — in *The Problems of Philosophy* — derides the phenomenon-noumenon split but he regards morals and aesthetics as coming ultimately from an unknown source. Wittgenstein, whose famous quote opens this chapter, is one of the few relatively modern philosophers who seems to have accepted that there is a hidden aspect to life for which we have no words.

Our true selves, the essence of who we are, also derives ultimately from mystery. The soul is the manifestation of that essence within an embodied person. The soul is the adventure of essence in the world. However, the adventure of essence can be frustrated by ego and personality and their tendency towards compulsion of all kinds. We will be exploring this in more detail as the work progresses.

4. Mind is split

'My one regret in life is not being born as somebody else'

Woody Allen

The split between phenomena and the noumenon is not just for the world 'out there'. It is not simply a boundary imposed on us in terms of getting empirical observations of the world. The split continues on from the objective world into the subjective world of consciousness. This is not the same as the splits identified by psychology such as ego, super ego and id or consciousness, sub-consciousness and collective consciousness. All of these divisions of the mind have their hidden aspects. Some of the psychological issues will be considered below, as these have a bearing on the development of the discussion within this work. But the phenomenon-noumenon split within the mind is treated as a further and distinct issue from the psychological concerns. As was observed in the previous chapter, modern philosophy — from the post-Kantian philosopher Schopenhauer onwards — has regarded subjects as having 'first person privilege', and with Schopenhauer at least, this is seen as some kind of inner knowledge of the workings of the noumenon.

Effectively, my will or volition is not really my own, it is the noumenon working through me.

The difficulty with Schopenhauer's first person privilege is that it might suggest that any and every thought and desire arising within me is actually the noumenon. Indeed, later philosophers, while dropping reference to the noumenon, have nonetheless taken up the idea that subjective thought and meaning are paramount in our view of reality and thus various forms of what we can loosely term 'new age' belief have been spawned.

However, a thought arising in consciousness is after all a phenomenon and therefore if we are to be consistent with our noumenon-phenomena split, then we would have to discard conscious thoughts as being directly attributable to the noumenon. A less direct approach is called for, as described below.

One of the most famous statements in philosophy is of course the 'Ergo Sum': 'I think, therefore I am'. Whilst not entirely new in Western thought, René Descartes' exposition of the idea really became the decisive point at which the subject/object split was adopted wholesale in Western thought. Being a subject moreover was not considered a complex issue. A thinking being was simply 'clear and precise'. Jean Paul Sartre, when commenting on the *ergo sum*, observed that the one doing the thinking is not necessarily the one observing the thought. He did not however comment further on this matter, but actually he hit the nail on the head with that observation. We must turn to Eastern thought and the idea of the 'witness' to help us to understand further.

In meditation, the process often known as 'the witness' is simply to stand back and to observe thoughts arising in the mind. A similar experience occurs when we find ourselves waking up in a strange place. The bed and immediate surroundings and sensations are brought into consciousness, but the unfamiliarity results in a few moments when we are unaware of who we are. These are usually moments of some alarm, as we struggle to find some reference of familiarity in order to 'ground' the self once again in the world. Essentially, it calls into question the nature of the self. If I can be fully conscious, yet unaware of who I am, then perhaps consciousness resides outside of myself or at least has levels or facets that can act discretely or independently. We might describe this as the noumenal consciousness, or our essence emanating from mystery. Just as we drew back from equating value with ultimate reality, I also want to draw back from equating all aspects of volition — all that might be described as 'the will' — with essence. Essence is mystery, and that is all that can be said.

If all is one, then of course, the witness and the self (or indeed essence and personality) are actually not separate. Some authors prefer to say that the self does not really exist, and that therefore all the problems relating to suppression and the sub-conscious are simply delusional. Only the noumenal consciousness is really real. We are however defined by the boundaries in which our lives are lived and to just ignore selves because ultimately they don't exist is I think not the best approach. In later chapters then, we will explore the self within the very deliberate context of the human economy.

We have noted already that to regard a 'subject', an individual thinking person, as a simple and clear concept, is to oversimplify. The process by which a person becomes a subject is fraught with difficulties. The splitting off of some aspects of the self into sub-conscious denial has serious consequences for the way we operate in the world.

Feminist author Grace Jantzen explains that Lacan assumes that language as constructed is essentially masculine. Women therefore effectively have no voice. Furthermore, language results in an endless deferral of desire (which Lacan describes as 'jouissance') and as being forever deferred. There is an endless search for substitute gratification. For Lacan, as for Freud, the phallus is the 'universal signifier'.

The split then, within the mind, in terms of a split that divides off the unconscious by the suppression of desire, has multiple consequences — a denial of genuine desire, the masculinity of Western thought, the suppression of the female, and the obsession with death. We will revisit these themes in later chapters. Jantzen and other feminist writers clearly feel that they must address these matters directly if they are to challenge the dominant mindset of psychology and find an alternative 'symbolic' — that is, a symbolic not related ultimately to the phallus. By way of a lead into this Jantzen turns to Levinas. She says:

'...whereas in psychoanalytic theory...speech and the whole of the cultural symbolic comes under the...phallus as the universal...signifier, Levinas situates speech otherwise. Speech as he understands it is not dominated by the phallus but as a response to the face, a face whose 'first word' is 'Thou shalt not kill.'

Levinas' work still presents difficulties for Jantzen, but the idea of embodiment (here exemplified in relating to others via the face) is very significant. Again, we will take up this theme later in the work.

Lawrence Cahoone (in *The Dilemma of Modernity*) identifies what he calls the 'three pernicious dichotomies' – the split between subject and object (mind and body, inner and outer), the split between the individual and the individual's relationships with others and the split between the world of human culture and the natural realm of biophysical processes. The last few chapters have looked at various splits in our world view, and the subject/object split has been a primary one. Cahoone's other splits, or dichotomies, relate closely to one another - more closely than might first appear. Hopefully this will become clear as the argument progresses and we will revisit Cahoone's dichotomies at the end of the work.

TWENTY-ONE LEVELS OF SELF-DECEPTION

5. Ascendancy and Descendancy

'...We seem not to have learned this lesson that the slimy body close at hand is holier that the dry distant mind, because we still pray to abstract gods and look beyond the sensuousness of the moment for redemption.'

Thomas Moore — Original Self

This work is divided into two sections, Eros and Agapé. The broader meaning of the terms and how they relate to the text is explained in the Introduction. Now we can equate these terms to another means by which the world is divided — 'ascendancy' and 'descendancy'. The ascendant aspect of life is mainly connected with Eros – although as we will see, it is in large part an Eros gone wrong. The descendant part of life is associated with Agapé. As explained in the Introduction, the term descendant is used advisedly — in truth this should be a horizontal relationship, but because our culture assumes a hierarchical, dominating stance, in this sense it might be seen as 'descent'. In terms of ultimate reality of course this is again a false split. Everything is both and none of these things. The division of the world into ascendancy and descendancy is a construct and a means of viewing the world in order to try to better understand it.

We make a further relation here by equating ascendancy with spirit and descendancy with soul. Both terms are of course loaded and can come with a lot of religious interpretations and perspectives. It is not the intention to use the terms in a religious or a spiritual sense in this work. Again, they are just tools for eliciting an understanding. Without their religious connotations, the two terms are nonetheless useful and informative. Our Western culture is greatly lacking in soul, it could be said. There is little respect for the notion of a life that seeks to be at home in the body and perhaps has a purpose distinct from our minds and egos. The notion sounds quite archaic to modern ears and perhaps somewhat self-indulgent. On the other hand, our culture has an interest in spirituality, as distinct from organised religion. This is somewhat complicated by the way these words have changed their meaning. The spirituality to which some in the West aspire is often better described as soulfulness, whilst the religion which is rejected is often not religious in the older sense of the word, but just a kind of formal and idealised spirituality.

Theism and pantheism also express this duality well — the one always aspiring to something which is forever beyond, whilst the other relates only to what is earth-bound. The middle way, 'panentheism', (as conceived by the German philosopher Kraus, amongst others) potentially recognises the aspects of ascendancy and descendancy and balances them both. Again, without necessarily ascribing to a religious perspective, these terms help us to understand this need for balance.

The two terms 'animus' and 'anima' also reflect the duality. *Animus* involves thought, judgement and heroics and relates to what we will henceforth describe as the 'economy of ascendancy'. *Anima* involves imagination, care-taking and depth of vision — we will describe this as the 'economy of descendancy'. The gendering of these terms is also highly significant (*animus* — male, *anima* — female).

'Deconstruction' in the manner of Derrida looks at binary oppositions, or polarities, with which Western philosophy has long been engaged. First it looks at emphasising the element of the binary that has historically been suppressed — Derrida was particularly interested in speech over writing and presence over absence. Then it moves on to look at the creative possibilities opened up by seeing beyond the binary opposition. We have been looking at such an opposition with regard to our economy of ascendancy and economy of descendancy — in which the latter is very much the suppressed. The next several chapters examine the economy of ascendancy and the economy of descendancy in more detail and examine the consequences of the suppression of descendancy.

6. Ascendancy is Spirit

'... if we want an intensification of spirituality, it might be better to become more intimate with the things of the earth than to build a self in the sky.'

> Thomas Moore — The Re-enchantment of Everyday Life

'The bodiless spirituality that many find comforting I don't trust.   I don't trust its preference for white light and its assumption that the spirit resides in the sky or in the brilliant stars.'

> Thomas Moore — Original Self

As explained in the previous chapter, the terms spirit and soul are used advisedly in this work – borrowed as they are from religion. Spirit is not used to mean that there is any kind of separate and discrete substance within a person that has its own existence. Nor do I subscribe to a literal belief that there is some element of God, such as the Holy Spirit, that can indwell an individual person and partly or fully motivate that person's actions.   The terms spirit and soul are often used almost interchangeably in religious writing.

I have chosen to ascribe particular aspects of our behaviour and of culture to each of the terms in order to try to draw out particular concerns. This apportioning as either 'spiritual' or 'soulful' is not entirely random! I am particularly indebted to the writings of Thomas Moore for identifying the relevance of the terms and applying them in a specific way. Of most importance is the relation of soul to body that we will explore in a later chapter and this is largely contrary to the understanding given to the word soul in its common religious usage.

I am deliberately staying with the terms spirit and soul in this work for two reasons. The first reason is that it continues with our theme of considering the splits within our thinking. We have noted that some splits go unnoticed almost entirely, others are recognised and seen as completely literal, whilst others still are recognised but misunderstood. Whilst considering that all splits are ultimately unreal, we can nevertheless use them in helping us to understand and perhaps challenge the status quo. The second reason for keeping with the terms spirit and soul is that although this is not essentially a religious work, nonetheless so much of what is said relates back to religion and to spirituality. Some authors, Hegel in particular, see genuine desire being met solely through religion, whilst others certainly acknowledge religious faith as being at least 'useful' in this regard. As the argument progresses we will see that unfortunately the way religion operates in the Western world unwittingly maintains and indeed reinforces the problems that this work seeks to illuminate and to challenge. Nonetheless, in seeking a community wherein people may find fulfilment of desire, compassion, well-being and flourishing, there may yet be hope that churches and spiritual groups can provide this. The 2012 'Occupy London' campaign, whose aims were perhaps not altogether clear and articulated, was nonetheless prescient in choosing St. Paul's Cathedral as the centre of their campaign. It was almost as if people were saying, society has failed us, values now need to come from elsewhere. Someone needs to help. That someone needs to be grounded elsewhere than in corporate greed and the politics of spin.

But this is to get ahead of ourselves. Let us return to the idea of spirit and start by looking at how it applies firstly within religion itself. Chapter 8 will explore how spirit — the economy of ascendancy — has come to dominate secular culture. In using the word religion, please take this to refer primarily to Western Christianity. This is mainly because this is the dominant religious influence in the West and its history is so much wrapped up in the development of philosophy, science and culture. I will however refer briefly to other faiths when this is relevant to the discussion.

Heaven is always above us and therefore always something to aspire to rather than something that is already with us. A more fundamentalist faith contrasts heaven not with Earth but with hell. The aspiration thus becomes all the more urgent. There is a strange kind of ambivalence in the image of heaven that is presented. On the one hand it is a wedding banquet — a celebration of all things physical — eating, drinking, marriage and love-making. On the other hand, these things seem often to be regarded as purely symbolic. Physicality is largely if not totally rejected. The perfection of human life, to which we are encouraged to aspire, is one of a disembodied spirit or soul, just as the nature of God is seen as 'pure' spirit. Heaven, in these terms, is therefore only reachable by death. It is in this sense that religion very much reinforces the general culture's obsession with and denial of death. The same ambivalence is played out in the way religion is presented. On the one hand it would claim to be life affirming. However, its chief image — the cross — is of an instrument of torture and death. People are always 'under' heaven and 'under' God, so we are locked into always having to aspire.

Desire is likewise misunderstood and thwarted. As we will explore later, it is in relationship with others that desire has the greatest potential to be realised. However, whilst this could be offered and embraced by religion, instead we are offered a substitute satisfaction for desire in the form of a 'relationship' with a being who is conceived as totally 'other' — pure spirit. The only way to reach this satisfaction of desire is to die and become pure spirit ourselves. In a traditional religious context there is an abstract notion of salvation. Creation spirituality writer Matthew Fox contrasts the sin/salvation approach of much of Western Christendom with the idea of atonement or 'at-one-ment'. God is with us instead of always above us, so there is a horizontal rather than a vertical relationship.

Grace Jantzen, whose work we mentioned in a previous chapter, speaks of religion which is too focused on personal spiritual journeys. She says:

'Religion can come adrift by becoming personal piety that gives observance and devotion so large a place that attention is deflected from the face of the other.
"Watch out for the peace of private worship! … the artificial peace of synagogues and churches!" It can come adrift in a focus on what might now be thought of as 'mysticism' or private religious experience, detached from justice: as Derrida recognises, such private ecstasy easily connives with every form of historical oppression.'

Indeed, the 'pious' — as John Gray (*Straw Dogs*) suggests, may actually be seeking to block out consciousness rather than to raise it to new heights. Perhaps the motive is to avoid seeing the world as it really is, in its vulnerability and its pain. Buddhism, despite recognising many of the problems inherent in religion, is still aspirational to an extent — with Nirvana or Enlightenment replacing heaven. The preoccupation with this world being essentially about suffering might also lead to an aspirational mindset. Mindfulness often involves focusing on the present moment — a moment that nonetheless is a moment of suffering. Whilst there is clearly benefit in recognising and not denying suffering there is nonetheless much in this world that is to be welcomed and enjoyed. There is a lot that is good about our embodiment and our lives in the here and now. Buddhists of course recognise the paradox. Aspiration towards a world free from desire is itself a desire. Despite Buddhism's emphasis on suffering, the meditation and silence seem to be good ways to allow a person to recognise and embrace real life rather than to flee from it, deny it or see it as sinful and compromised. Meditation and silence are a means of letting go.

The ascendant makes use of image or representation as part of its aspiration. Of course heaven itself is a very powerful image above all else, whether it is regarded as a projection of earthly values into a rarefied form or some kind of realm of pure spirit (whatever that might mean). Spirituality more generally might aspire to a notion of perfect peace but conceived of as some kind of perfect state rather than as an acknowledgement that of course we are already 'at one' so in fact have no journey to undertake.

Our culture is also spiritual in a more general way in that it is unfailingly aspirational. The aspirations now however are more to do with evolution and the search for a 'theory of everything' in science, materialism and infinite economic growth in politics and career, comfort and body image in the personal realm. We are a culture that is always looking for progress and not content just to be. This will be explored in Chapter 8.

Ascendancy fails to recognise any boundaries. Ascendancy needs to be balanced with the 'descendent' aspects of life. There needs to be an economy of descendancy that recognises and sets limits on the tendency of Eros to seek unrealisable goals. The energy of Eros needs to be channelled into the reality of our embodiment.

7. Descendancy is Soul

'Our soul is everything — mediating between our personality and our essence, and part of both...'

Simon Parke — The Beautiful Life

As discussed in the Introduction, the term descendancy is used in order to describe those aspects of life that I am suggesting represent its soulfulness. It might be more appropriate to say that the soul reaches out to body and nature rather than reaches down (as implied by descendancy). Descendancy however is being used to contrast with ascendancy. We are already 'down' as it were, but we often do not recognise this. Again, it is to employ the method of contrasting a polarity in thinking and to look at what happens when the less-favoured of the binary oppositions is given prominence. What does it mean to favour soul over spirit or descendancy over ascendancy?

The attributes of ascendancy are largely regarded as male attributes and those of descendancy as female. Wisdom — *'Sophia'* — of course is also feminine. It is in the economy of descendancy that we find wisdom. In previous chapters we have identified concerns with the dominant ascendant attributes in philosophy, religion, science and culture. Much of this can be attributed to an underlying male-domination in the way that Western thought has developed. The feminine has been suppressed and given no voice. As a result, both women and men have suffered.

The centrality and importance of the soul — now so often neglected by our modern dualistic societies – is well expressed by Thomas Moore:

'Throughout history the soul has been discussed in a trinitarian context where mind and body find their humanity in a third place, the soul, where behaviour and belief are deepened in imagination, and where emotion and mind join in intelligent, deeply felt values.'

> Thomas Moore — *The Re-enchantment of Everyday Life*

W.B. Yeats says simply: 'There is only one history, and that is the soul's.' Likewise, Simon Parke, in his book *The Beautiful Life*, emphasises the essential but neglected importance of the soul:

'The soul is not given ... It is a creation with endless variation of shape and nature, which starts with a desire in your mind, and can become anything.'

And again:

'...when we use the word soul, we use it to describe a cascading waterfall of experience, all power and fluidity, all change and force, all energy and life, a crashing vastness of possibility and engaged at every level of our physical and psychological well-being.'

> Both quotes from Simon Parke — *The Beautiful Life*

The soul is essentially quite happy to immerse itself in nature and is not that interested in any kind of 'development'.

Meister Eckhart says:

'The soul loves the body.'

(Contrast this with St. Augustine: 'The soul makes war with the body.')

Meister Eckhart again:-

'The soul is not in the body, but the body is in the soul.' And Meister Eckhart further tells us: 'Our souls grow by subtraction not by addition.' Learning, or a self-directed program of 'spiritual growth' might detract rather than enhance the soul. The distractions of wealth, work and possessions may not satisfy our souls and therefore ultimately not satisfy our true selves. In fact any kind of holding onto things - be they material things or beliefs or attitudes — can be a problem. There needs rather to be a letting go on the one hand and on the other hand a creative engagement with others and with the world around us. Thomas Moore again:

'The soul needs to be fattened, not explained, and certain things are nutritious, whilst others are without taste or benefit. Good food for the soul includes especially anything that promotes intimacy; a hike in nature, a late-night conversation with a friend, a family dinner, a job that satisfies deeply, a visit to a cemetery. Beauty, solitude and deep pleasure also keep the soul well fed.'

> Thomas Moore — *The Re-enchantment of Everyday Life*

The soul thrives on dreams and imagination. Thomas Moore again:

'The soul has an absolute, unforgiving need for regular excursions into enchantment.'

'... the soul craves charm and fascination. Its natural emotions are longing, desire, interest, attachment, surprise, and pleasure, as well as darker feelings of melancholy, fear, loss, envy, jealousy and anger.'

> Both quotes from Thomas Moore — *The Re-enchantment of Everyday Life*

And according to Joanna Macey (*The Work that Re-Connects*) the future is:

'...not constructed by our minds as much as to emerge from our dreams...We will never be able to build what we have not first cherished in our hearts.'

Even authors with no particular religious or spiritual intent make use of the idea of the soul to illustrate our situation as human beings. Take this quote from psychologist Alexander Lowen:

'A person who does not feel he is part of a larger scheme, that does not sense that his life is part of a natural process that is bigger than himself, can be said to be without a soul.'

Alexander Lowen — *Pleasure*

Lowen continues:

'If he has a soul, a man can break through the narrow boundaries of the self and can experience the joy and ecstasy of oneness with the universal. If he doesn't have a soul, a man is locked in the prison of his mind and his pleasures are limited to ego satisfactions.'

When we considered the ascendant, spirit side of life, we noted that in many aspects of culture and in religion there is an abstract goal to which we might aspire. Often this abstract goal is associated with a representation or image. The abstract goals and associated image are often not recognised as being unrealisable, as we saw in an earlier chapter. The emphasis in Part 2 of this work will be how we can dig down into life. How do we make the ideals and aspirations of spirit manifest in the real world? How do we acknowledge and fulfil genuine desire? How do we bring soul back into life, by understanding our embodiment and our place in nature and by honouring instead of suppressing the feminine? How do we balance Eros and Agapé — ascendancy and descendancy?

I hope that it is obvious that there is a very decisive split between the aspiration of spirit on the one hand and the needs of the soul on the other. Both our contemporary culture and much of organised religion in the West reflect the ideals of the economy of ascendancy. By contrast, Thomas Moore tells us:

'The soul does not evolve or grow... Its odyssey is a drifting at sea, a floating toward home, not an evolution toward perfection.'

Thomas Moore — *Original Self*

The contrast between our two economies, ascendancy and descendancy, are further explored by Matthew Fox. Fox, instead of contrasting spirit and soul, contrasts 'Jacob's ladder' with 'Sarah's circle'. A Jacob's ladder style of thinking and acting is characterised by:

1. Up/Down.
2. Flat Earth (A Monist, reductionist view of life).
3. Climbing (aspirational, economy of ascendancy).
4. Sisyphian (ie, trying to push things up the ladder).
5. Competitive.
6. Restrictive and elitist (survival of the fittest).
7. Hierarchical.
8. Violent.
9. Sky-orientated (aspiring to abstract goals).
10. Ruthlessly independent.
11. Jealous and judgement-orientated.
12. Abstract, distant-making.
13. Linear, ladder-like.
14. Theistic (immanent or transcendent).
15. Love of neighbour is separated from love of what is at the top.

We have considered some of these points in our chapters on ascendancy. We can note here though the jealous, competitive, ruthless, violent and judgmental characteristics that Fox mentions — all very much related to the male-dominated nature of western civilisation. Contrast this (point by point) with Sarah's circle thinking:

1. In/Out. (We may best understand this as horizontal relations, as opposed to the Up/Down of Jacob's ladder.)
2. Global village (recognising and embracing diversity).
3. Dancing, celebrating.
4. Satisfying.
5. Shared ecstasies.
6. Welcoming, non-elitist (survival of all).
7. Democratic.
8. Strong and gentle.
9. Earth-orientated.
10. Interdependent.
11. Pride-producing, non-judgmental.
12. Nurturing and sensual.
13. Curved, circle-like.
14. Panentheistic (transparent).
15. Love of neighbour *is* love of God.

We will be exploring some of these points in future chapters. In particular the meaning of panentheism is of relevance to our discussion, as is the contrasting points 15 in the two scenarios Fox presents. The soul recognises its context in nature and in the body. Its relation to both is generally one of delight. The economy of descendancy recognises the economy of ascendancy and can act as a corrective to the tendency of spirit to aim for abstract goals. The economy of ascendancy fails to recognise the economy of descendancy or tries to reframe it as some kind of 'spirituality'.

8. Ascendancy dominates

'I know the untameable spirit of man; bent it cannot be - but it can be broken.'

Seneca the Younger — Thyestes

Society's state is essentially a state of denial. Society aspires to some form of progress — evolution, ongoing economic growth, eventual conquest of all of nature — in order to maintain our species forever with ever-receding horizons of achievement. Both science and religion unwittingly conspire in promoting these kinds of aspiration, which is essentially pure spirit – the 'economy of ascendancy'. Both have equally lost sight of our origins in the Earth and the celebration of our physical existence. Both lack soul — the 'economy of descendancy'. A consistent pattern of the economy of ascendancy is the setting up of an image or an ideal that we then strive to achieve. The problem is that these images or ideals are often impossible to realise. A good and happy life is always just out of reach — might not in fact ever be realised until we die. We will see a little of how this is played out in this chapter and visit this theme again later in the work.

On a personal level, we face a similar dilemma

to that faced by society at large. The outward, expansionist view of life (health, career, material affluence, body image) denies that ultimately these things will fail. Too much investment in them therefore is to live in denial (and perhaps also in fear). It is better to acknowledge our limits, to find what we really want to do within the context of these limits and to invest in this, rather than invest in abstract, unrealisable goals. There is also much that we need to let go of. The economy of descendancy is better placed to come to these realisations, as we will explore in future chapters.

Western philosophy has traditionally been largely dominated by metaphysics and epistemology — theories about existence and knowledge over and above theories about relationship. This is a further pattern of the economy of ascendancy and again we will return to it later in the work.

Science, by its own lights, regards itself as having a purely 'rational' view of the world. It would therefore deny any underlying desire that motivates what is researched for instance and the way the results of research are presented and crucially, how the information gained is applied in technology. We can note that science is predominantly 'monist' in that it reduces everything to one substance — matter. The fact that some matter forms itself into living beings is still a largely mysterious process. But the 'solution' at the moment seems to be to reduce biology to chemistry and chemistry to physics. Consciousness is described as an epi-phenomenon — a side effect of a purely physical process. We might suggest that the underlying desire in all this is for power over nature.

Science adopted the concept of evolution wholesale and whilst the 'survival of the fittest' version has become increasingly discredited, there is still an underlying assumption that evolution inevitably implies progress. There are still works that suggest the further evolution of humans to some kind of superhuman creature. Of course now that process is 'helped' by technology rather than as a result of natural environments. We are on dangerous ground.

Science also has an inherent belief that everything is solvable and ultimately understandable by the accumulation of knowledge and by reasoning. Hence the search for the elusive 'theory of everything' in physics. If it were ever found it would not really be a theory of everything — it would simply be a way of describing the actions of sub-atomic particles that would perhaps relate to physics and chemistry in the macro world. It would be a theory of everything only in as much as you believe reality to be made up of lumps of dead matter.

Culture uses representation in politics — an ideology serves as an image of a perfect state. More recent politics has become somewhat more subtle — has a covert rather than an overt ideology — but nonetheless uses image to fuel aspiration. The main aspiration in Western consumer capitalism is economic growth. Somehow this is seen as being an ultimate 'solution' to all ills. If only a society can grow in economic terms, it is argued, then all else will follow. Western politics deals a lot with desire, but they are substitute desires. Politics either knowingly or unwittingly plays into the fact that individuals are largely unconscious of their underlying desire and will therefore seek substitutes via materialism, career and so on. At best, governments might hope to achieve human well-being and flourishing — the fulfilment of genuine desire — as some kind of after-effect of having material needs met. There is also still a denial of death, but this plays out tellingly in the 'rights' afforded to individuals. 'Freedom' is paramount in liberal democracy, and with that comes the protection of private property, protection from the threat of violence inflicted by other citizens or violence and war occurring from outside the particular nation. These may seem like worthy aims, but they are all premised on the idea that there are restraints, threats and danger at every turn. The kind of freedom on offer is a freedom external to the self and bought with the threat of violence. Such a system is in the end life-denying rather than life-affirming.

The image of the body is likewise prevalent in Western culture. The body is 'objectified' — given extrinsic value. The image of the perfect body then becomes an abstract ideal towards which men and women strive. We strive perhaps towards an ideal for our own bodies. Perhaps we also strive to find a relationship and sexual fulfilment via an image of the body in others. Of course, the owners of bodies are also persons! Hence, when confronted by the personhood of others then the response may be ambiguous. Perhaps we will see beyond the image and find a more satisfying whole person, but perhaps we will feel disillusioned. Real desire is tied up intimately with the body and the idea of body image comes close to recognising this, but still ends up as a substitute desire. We are first and foremost embodied persons. Fulfilment of desire is more to do with relating to other embodied persons rather than some kind of endless aspiration toward good looks. The body image aspiration treats bodies essentially as commodities — as another material possession. So, whilst obsessed with the body in one sense, our culture is also at the same time in denial of the body.

The problem is neatly summarised in this quote from Thomas Moore:

'We seem to be always reaching for an elusive goal, rather than loving the world in front of our eyes, just as we put anxious effort into becoming a new person, instead of loving and living the life we've always had and always will have.'

> Thomas Moore — *The Re-enchantment of Everyday Life*

In a similar vein, Carl Jung said that there are two ways to lose your soul and one is to worship a god outside of you.

All of this is not to say that image and representation are necessarily bad things. Imagination, creativity, dreams, hopes — all of these rely on image almost by definition. Matthew Fox — rather than speak of image — speaks of 'signs' and 'symbols'. A sign, for him, is a very specific and thereby controlling image.

A symbol on the other hand, is much more free, giving us guidance and inspiration, such as in imagination, dreams and fantasies. The problem lies in trying to translate an image or symbol into a living reality. How is salvation to become a lived reality? How is spirituality made manifest in the particulars of real life? How can science be applied with compassion? How can political ideals manifest as genuine social justice? How can body image enhance personhood rather than be at odds with it? These questions are key to our argument as it is developed in later chapters.

Before moving on to explore the economy of descendancy, some last words from Thomas Moore:

'If we continue to transform all nations of the world into homogenised, high-tech….. all-function cultures of disenchantment, we will have few unique spirits left to nourish our souls. We will be a people without ghosts and without things to house those ghosts, a people so bereft of spirituality in everyday things that we will turn, as many already have, to outrageous otherworldly venues for our spiritual experiences. This truly will be a dangerous time, because human community and civility are not, as some would say, humanistic achievements; they are the work of the ghosts of memory and the spirit of place, of the genius in things and the soul of culture.

> Thomas Moore — *The Re-enchantment of Everyday Life*

Abstract 'representational' aims are accepted

without question. The possibility of alternatives is not even considered. An abstract goal has no possibility of fulfilment. It is only because heaven or Nirvana, the theory of everything, the perfect political state and the perfect body are unrealisable that we often fail to see the pointlessness of the endless striving involved.

No boundaries are acknowledged by the ascendant culture. But all of the various elements discussed above should have their respective boundaries. For science we might recognise a self-imposed boundary. We might describe it as the 'boundary of ecology'. Wherever science crosses the boundary of what damages rather than serves the ecosystem it should be restrained. There should likewise be a boundary in politics – sustainability and the well-being and flourishing of people. The human economy would in turn be bounded by the ecological boundary mentioned above. Along with science, no other human activity should inflict damage on the ecosystem of which we are a part. Finally there is a boundary set by our embodiment. Spirituality itself (the limitless aspirations to Eros) needs to be bounded by the reality of our embodiment. The dignity of our personhood should never be compromised by seeing either ourselves or others as mere 'objects'. Genuine desire is satisfied rather than frustrated by this boundary, as will be explored in a later chapter.

Part 2 - Agapé

9. The world is disenchanted

The beginning of wisdom in any human activity is a certain reverence for the primordial mystery of existence.'

Thomas Berry — The Dream of the Earth

The main split in this work is between Eros and Agapé. It should be clear by now that the balance between these two is out of kilter. Nevertheless, both are needed. The dividing line in this work is therefore something of an arbitrary one. Whilst it is stressed that the economy of descendancy needs more attention, Eros still requires its rightful place. Ken Wilber speaks of the balance between the two:

'...Phobos is Eros without Agapé (transcendence without embrace, negation without preservation).

'And Phobos drives the mere Ascenders.

'In their frantic wish for an "other world", their ascending Eros strivings, otherwise appropriate, are shot through with Phobos, with ascetic repression, with a denial, a fear and a hatred of anything "this-worldly", a denial of vital life, of sexuality, of sensuality, of nature, of body (and always of women).

'...Thanatos, on the other hand is Descent divorced from Ascent...
'...Thanatos is Agapé without Eros.
'And Thanatos drives the mere Descenders.'

Ken Wilber — *Sex, Ecology, Spirituality*

In Chapter 1 we mentioned the 'disqualified universe' - a view of the world that is stripped of all value judgements. Wikipedia defines it thus:

'...disenchantment... is the cultural rationalisation and devaluation of mysticism apparent in modern society. The concept was borrowed from Friedrich Schiller by Max Weber to describe the character of modernised, bureaucratic, secularised western society, where scientific understanding is more highly valued than belief and where processes are orientated towards rational goals as opposed to traditional society, where for Weber "the world remains a great enchanted garden."'

(Wikipedia quotes from Max Weber — *The Sociology of Religion*)

But the disenchanted world is in fact just a pretence. Values still lurk just beneath the surface in both individuals and in culture generally and have an even more insidious grip for going unacknowledged. There is a rejection of things that suggest some kind of value — at odds with an apparent acceptance of all values that we might assume should be the stance of a tolerant society. At the same time, Western culture also seems to embrace truth as an ultimate value and quite readily speculates on truth as being transcendent. Mathematical 'forms' are regarded as somehow pre-existent or transcendent and yet such a notion would be rejected wholesale if it were suggested for beauty. Only the religious perhaps maintain a belief in transcendent goodness.

Modernism and post-modernism sit awkwardly side by side therefore and present us with a double standard of truth. Modernism still clings to a transcendent truth of science and mathematics and yet at the same time argues for relativity in all other aspects of truth. We can somehow have a personal subjective truth that is okay for us so long as it does not overlap any scientific truth. Likewise, goodness and beauty are seen as subjective, but there is a rejection of strongly-held values as well as a rejection of beauty for its own sake that might be expressed in sensuality. There is a common disregard for the 'sensualist' in art, perhaps exemplified by criticisms of neo-classicism. This seems strange and contradictory in an intellectual environment that usually purports to be post-modern. A broader aesthetic that might find expression in a bohemian or decadent lifestyle may also be questioned.

We only have the liberty of such ambivalence because of centuries of struggle in the West. Modernism has fought to separate science, art and theology as well as promote democracy and equality. Church, State, Monarchy and the Law can all act independently. This permits us the freedom to express whatever we like in words and pictures without fear of being branded either a traitor or a blasphemer or both. The Monarchy cannot stand above the Law. The Church can hold theological and moral precepts of its own, but cannot enforce them via the State — and so on. Perhaps most of us do not stop to think what a privilege this situation is and how genuinely unique in terms of the history of human civilisations and cultures. There are still relatively few countries in the world where such freedom is even understood, let alone permitted. However, those hard-won freedoms of Western culture come with a heavy price. We are rudderless and ambivalent as a society, and often in denial.

What are we to make of this? Thomas Moore reminds us of the overarching wildness and mystery from which we have come:

'Mystery is not a vague unknown; it is a specific unknowable... Contemporary western life is often split into frenetic passions and emotions that break out destructively in city streets and in family homes, and an endless supply of explanations, interpretation, and solutions is offered. What is missing here is the soul, evoked by an archetypal imagination in which the passions and the imagination combine in an alchemy that generates our humanity.'

> Thomas Moore — *The Re-enchantment of Everyday Life*

As Moore suggests, this lack of soulfulness and the ambiguity is made manifest by peculiarities in our culture. On the surface, everything is very ordered, clean, tidy and efficient, but underneath all is not so well. On occasion, 'chaos' breaks out. There are substitute gratifications such as material wealth and power. There is an obsession with the image of death, but a denial of death itself. There is an obsession with the image of the body, but a denial of the body itself. There is an obsessional belief in individual freedom, but we protect that freedom with the threat of extreme violence. There is an obsession with sport, an obsession with celebrity, a compulsion toward status, a compulsion toward fixing trivial problems whilst global concerns are ignored or denied. There are outpourings of emotion over relatively inconsequential matters whilst war, famine and pollution continue to wreak havoc. There is a strange 'shadow life' of internet trolls, paedophiles, misogynists, racists, homophobics and religious fundamentalists, whilst outwardly society claims to be equal and tolerant. All of this, I suggest, is a clinging to things — both materially, emotionally and subjectively. Clinging onto 'stuff'. Fear of old age and death. Fear of not looking attractive. Fear of our own bodies. Fear that other lifestyles and other views will force us to re-evaluate our own lives. The holding onto paranoid and aggressive views whilst at the same time maintaining a 'front' of reasonableness and tolerance. All of this speaks of a society that is psychotic.

Perhaps there is good reason for people to seek escape in various ways from lives and routines that have become mind-numbingly predictable. But the various forms of 'escape' that are sought lack any clear direction. Creativity is frustrated. We have tamed the inner wildness of ourselves, because of our culture's taming of the outer wildness of nature. So, our efforts at creativity are trivialised. Perhaps then, 'obscene' graffiti speaks to us about an eroticism that we fail to give adequate expression to in our culture.

Wildness, walled in, will seek whatever means available to find its expression. Wildness is the domain of soul -the adventure of essence in the world. We need to claim this word soul back for ourselves and re-evaluate the place of soul in all aspects of our lives.

Western culture thinks that a subjective, soulful, enchanted view of life is somehow just fanciful and irrelevant. The desire-driven, body-centred, imaginative and creative aspects of our lives – in which we should be taking delight - are denied to us almost from birth by a culture that disparages such things as being superficial, self-indulgent and psychotic. Culture however is in denial of desire. Genuine desire is thwarted and replaced by power over and power under dynamics and the substitute desires of materialism, wealth and status.

What we have identified as the ascendant view of life is seen as the only possible view. This view recognises no boundaries in terms of knowledge of a world that is regarded as solely material and objective. The ascendant view of life also sees no boundary in potential power and control over nature. An economy of descendancy would see the erotic expressed through relationship between embodied persons and between persons and the ecosystem of which we form a part. It would perceive Agapé as the community in which such relationships would be nurtured and sustained. Imagination and creativity would recover proper focus.

10. Desire leads us

Now and then its good to pause in our pursuit of happiness and just be happy.

Guillaume Apollinaire

Here, and throughout this work, I have made a distinction between genuine desire and substitute desires. I use genuine desire in the sense of something very basic and fundamental to our consciousness. It is genuine desire or ecstasy that is said to be lost and denied early in childhood and results in the sub-conscious and in substitute desires. Desires are simply pleasures that stand in – usually unconsciously — as compensations for the genuine desire that has been suppressed and denied. Desire is the image of pleasure. Just as we saw images set up for other ideas — in religion, in politics and in our relationship with our bodies — so there are images for pleasure that are false images and lead us away from genuine desire. Therefore to talk about desire leads us into having an abstract goal that then instigates an unending pursuit for the unobtainable. We will talk mainly of pleasure henceforth. Nevertheless, we will want to distinguish between pleasures that are compensatory and are pursued as individualistic sensations and those pleasures that are grounded in relationship with others, with the wildness of nature and ultimately with mystery.

According to Antonio Damasio, emotions are essentially the bridge between mind and body. The mind/body, subject/object split is so central to Western thought that it is difficult to conceive of any kind of continuity between the two worlds. Damasio himself has gone to great effort to challenge what has become the 'common sense' view of reality, best articulated by Descartes. He reminds us of the legacy of a more unified philosophy, exemplified, in his view, by Spinoza.

Very often the body is much more connected with what is really going on in our lives and indeed far more adept at knowing what would be best for us in terms of our short-term and long-term happiness. The body 'remembers' our genuine pleasure therefore. However, Western culture has put far more emphasis on mind. As such, to our minds, our body's attempts to communicate to us via emotion and physicality can appear to be random or confusing or are simply ignored and suppressed.

Ego fears looking silly. Ego regards itself as wholly rational. It fails to see that emotions such as envy, pride and fear play a big part in its decision-making process or that genuine desire underlies its presumed rationality, but is itself suppressed.

Theologian Grace Jantzen says this:

'Desire is both the indispensable substantiation of rationality and its danger; it is the *other* of rationality. By setting up rationality and desire as alterities, indeed as separate functions and attributes, it becomes impossible ... to speak of rational desires or desirable rationality. The self is radically fractured into a binary opposition of the rational and the irrational, familiar since Plato. But whereas passion and desire have traditionally been conceptually linked within the irrational (and with the female and the body) ... desire also subtends the rational even while [passion and desire] are rationality's other and its source of danger.'

> Grace M. Jantzen — *Becoming Divine* (author's emphasis).

In other words there is pleasure rooted and underling our attempts at rationality but rationality itself denies pleasure.

There are various ways then that mind and emotions get confused and with that our understanding of where pleasure might lie. Without resorting to therapy, how are we to uncover these matters and see and understand our reactions to people and events? How do we reach our genuine pleasure?

In *The Art of Being*, Erich Fromm suggests four ways in which we can help ourselves towards a deeper understanding of our own nature. Paraphrasing, these are:

1. Examining thoughts which occur when you are trying to remain still.
2. If feeling angry or tired, try to dig down into what might be the genuine cause of these feelings, rather than their superficial cause.

[Jung spoke of the 'shadow'. Sometimes we have a strong reaction to something we observe in another person, but quickly ignore it or cannot explain it.]

3. Still another approach is an autobiographical one … speculation about one's history, beginning with one's early childhood and ending with one's projected future development. Try to get a picture of significant events, of your early fears, hopes, disappointments, events that decreased your trust and faith in people, and in yourself. Ask: On whom am I dependent? What are my main fears? What were my goals in the past and what are they now? What is my image of myself? What is the image I wish others to have of me? Are there discrepancies between the two images? Is either image the same as my real self? Who will I be if I continue to live as I am living now? What are the alternatives for the future open to me now? Could I live differently?

4. Ask if you have an 'official' version of what your life is about, which is the mask you present to the world. How does this contrast with the 'real' version of what your life is truly about and what really motivates you.

All of these methods, but in particular the last one, are means by which we can know the real motivations in our lives, the fears that we may cling to and how we might realise genuine pleasure. Fromm is suggesting mainly looking at fears and problems, unravelling their root cause as a means of then letting these things go. The image others might have of us is also a means toward achieving this. We are not being asked simply to create a better image of ourselves, either for our own sakes or to present to others. We are at least being asked to present a more honest image. Ultimately, we are just looking for an 'unveiling', an openness to the world. This in turn allows for pleasures that are not simply superficial distractions. We might also describe Fromm's suggestions as self-disruption — a deliberate stepping back from the normal flow of thoughts and impressions. Troubles and misfortunes - provided not deliberately sought — can also perform this task. Problems can be turned around into opportunities to know ourselves and to see where letting go may be appropriate.

The oneness of ultimate reality has led some to suggest that there really is no self. The notion of an individual self is just an illusion; therefore, it is suggested, there's no reason to worry or to investigate the inner workings of the mind or emotions. Within the economy of human affairs however, the self is undeniable. So, whilst realising it is ultimately a delusion, a certain amount of effort seems justified in exploring our own inner space. We could also say that whilst the self might ultimately be an illusion, consciousness is not! The wonder of being is known as much within ourselves as by looking outward to nature. Knowing ourselves is also the beginning of compassion. It is a mistake to think that we can love nature and other human beings without first loving and accepting ourselves.

Psychoanalysis now seems obsessed with examining desire, especially personal desire and how this can be gratified or frustrated. By contrast, much of what we have looked at in terms of self-awareness is to do with examining the negatives in our lives and how these can be let go. The search for happiness and the fulfilment of desire somehow needs less examination. It will always be there as a cascading waterfall, a never-ending flood of new adventures. To examine this in any detail is perhaps to cut off its vigour and its mystery — to try to tame desire is ultimately like trying to tame a tiger — foolish and pointless.

All we need to realise pleasure is acceptance and honesty. We do not need to be afraid of who we really are — we need to be able to tell ourselves and others where our true pleasures lie. To really bring this home we might say: I am my pleasure; I am the object of my pleasure. Our self and genuine pleasure are intimately linked. Knowing yourself is the only way to know pleasure and the only way to satisfy it. Also, it must be the starting point for genuine compassion.

So our societies have a confused view of things, thinking that pleasure is some kind of self-indulgent added extra to life rather than central to it. In this we are denying our true motivations and thinking that we live our lives primarily as rational beings rather than embodied and emotional, pleasure-driven persons. The economy of descendancy that harmonises the aspirations of spirit with soulfulness, recognises that we are embodied persons, understands genuine pleasure and seeks its fulfilment within interbeing and compassion.

11. Desire is always ambiguous

'I desire to press in my arms the loveliness which has not yet come into the world.'

James Joyce — Portrait of the Artist as a Young Man

In Chapter 9, we looked briefly at some of the ambiguities that arise from our culture's lack of soulfulness. There are substitute gratifications such as material wealth, power and status. There is an obsession with the image of death, but a denial of death itself. There is an obsession with the image of the body, but a denial of the body itself. There is an obsessional belief in individual freedom, but we protect that freedom with the threat of extreme violence. There is a strange 'shadow life' of extremist views whilst outwardly society claims to be equal and tolerant. All of this, I suggest, is a clinging to things — both materially, emotionally and subjectively. The main thing that we hold onto is fear.

As we have touched on already, genuine pleasure is suppressed in us even as we become fully conscious of ourselves as separate subjects. Unfortunately, the very notion of being a subject in Western thought is deeply associated with death and with a divisive split between male and female. In order to become a 'subject', certain desires must be repressed and rationalised. What is more, Western thought has conceived this in purely masculine terms (Freud and Lacan). Women, in this view, only become subjects by being man-like. Any attempt at equality therefore is fated, as the 'equality' can only be constructed within these phallocentric terms.

How to escape from this dilemma? Let us first just summarise what such an escape might mean. It means a fully equal place to the feminine in both men and women. It means life over death. It means discerning genuine pleasure over substitute and superficial pleasures. It means the freedom to let go of any number of things and to allow creativity to flourish. Ultimately, it is the interplay of form (creativity) and formlessness (letting go). However, as we'll see, there is a point at which the flow and counterflow meet each other — where there will always be paradox.

True freedom, for the economy of ascendancy — for spirit — only comes about after bodily death. There is therefore an implicit embrace of death underlying all of Western culture's aspirations. Therefore, in order to find freedom via our alternative economy of descendancy we must set up a symbolic that challenges this world view – something that will 'bring to rest the ceaselessly shifting signifiers' – the ever-receding horizon of substitute pleasures by fulfilling genuine pleasure. In Martin Luther King's words, we must find something to love more than death. *All of our delusions hide us from this central fact. To love something more than death is ultimately a perfect summary of the intentions of this work.*

Grace Jantzen further comments on this obsession with death:

'...the western intellectual tradition is obsessed with death and with other worlds, a violent obsession that is interwoven with a masculinist drive for mastery... a deconstructive examination of this emphasis on death shows that it has an unacknowledged foundation, a material and maternal foundation in natality, which is precisely what is threatening to a masculinist imaginary, but without which none of the rest could proceed.'

She goes on to look at the implications of acknowledging the centrality of natality over death:

'I suggest that much of traditional philosophy of religion (and western culture generally) is preoccupied with violence, sacrifice and *death*, and built upon mortality not only as a human fact but as a fundamental philosophical category. But what if we were to begin with *birth*, and with the hope and possibility and wonder implicit in it? How if we were to treat natality and the emergence of *this* life and *this* world with the same philosophical seriousness and respect which had traditionally been paid to mortality and the striving for other worlds?'

Grace M. Jantzen — *Becoming Divine* (Author's emphases)

Our economy of descendancy is best placed therefore to redress the balance. In particular, our hopes should lie with the feminine in all aspects of life.

We have talked though of a certain ambiguity that is inherent in all of this process. I suggest now that this ambiguity is most apparent in our relation to the cosmos, to nature and to our own inner nature. As the earlier chapters of this work hopefully made clear, the apparent contradiction at the level of the universe — form and formlessness — is only resolved by the ultimate unity of all things — nonduality. This in turn is reflected in the wildness of nature — a wildness that we somehow cannot wuite accept and therefore seek to tame. And the wildness of nature is right within us, in our own bodies and in our minds and souls. The essence of who we are is wildness. In sexuality in particular, and sexual desire, these contradictions come to the fore. Furthermore this is not a contradiction that needs to be 'solved' or 'resolved' in some way. For ourselves, as embodied persons, it is — or could be — a cause for celebration, as we see the paradox of all of nature played out in our own lives. Thomas Moore says this:

'Desire is the proper atmosphere of the sexual kingdom. It keeps us alive and moving along. It keeps us in touch with memories, warm and sad, and it allows us entry to the world of imagination when all around us practicality is insistent. *From the viewpoint of the soul, desire simply is; it need not be satisfied....*
'The little desires are connected to and call forth the bigger ones... And so every desire is worth paying attention to, even though we know that

if we track it far enough, we will discover that this longing will never cease. But that is the definition of divinity from the viewpoint of sexuality. That full, bittersweet, empty feeling is like incense in a church — it announces the presence of God.

'... Sexuality certainly brings people together and makes life feel full and vital. But it is also the path toward that extreme of desire, that ultimate love that usually feels unrequited, which is the eternal and the infinite. The opening made by desire, that hole in our satisfaction, is the opening to divinity, and only there is our desire brought into the realm of the possible.'

> Thomas Moore — *Original Self* (My emphasis)

These experiences of ceaseless desire and unrequited desire are indeed significant ones, as Moore suggests. We reach out to create pleasure in the world. We create form but at the same time move towards formlessness. It is the essential paradox at the centre of ourselves and at the centre of all that exists. The oneness of all is form and formlessness, and neither and both.

In knowing ourselves, we learn to let go. In this sense, we move toward formlessness. But, in reaching for pleasure, we create form. It is the awe at the beauty of the world and other people that inspires us. And it is ultimately beauty that we seek to create in being pleasure for others.

Therefore we are deluded to think that pleasure can be fulfilled in some absolute way — either in another life or by some kind of substitute satisfaction of material wealth, power or status. An alternative symbolic — birth and becoming — help us to realise this goal. However, in our encounters with wild nature and the wildness within ourselves — our bodies, our souls — we encounter the paradox of the creative force of the universe and its reciprocal. We experience both form and formlessness. Such desire is always paradoxical - it can never really be satisfied. But that is how things should be. Grand notions of ultimate fulfilment are just visions of an impossible heaven.

12. Meaning will always allude us

'Don't seek the truth — just shed your opinions.'

Japanese Zen Master

If the true nature of reality is mystery, then it is difficult to see how any meaning could ever be discerned or understood. There may well be such a meaning, but by definition it is unknowable. Mircea Eliade says: 'When something sacred manifests itself (hierophany), [that is, if we catch a glimpse of transcendent meaning] at the same time something "occults" itself, becomes cryptic. Therein lies the true dialectic of the sacred: by the mere fact of *showing* itself, the sacred *hides* itself.' Since we do not know whether there is any meaning or not then life will of necessity be ambiguous and to some extent conflicted.

I would suggest then that the search for a transcendent meaning is really the problem rather than the solution. We look for meaning for ourselves, or at least to appropriate meaning, by looking outside of ourselves. We look for some objective truth that will centre meaning in our lives — perhaps backing up that truth with religious conviction. In a sense, we aim at an image of meaning — rather like the way we might aim at an image of spirituality, ideological politics or body image. Simon Parke takes up this idea:

'So we shall not strive for truth, for there is no need. Indeed, it has been said that it is best not to strive for anything, for striving is concerned with goals, and there are no goals, for you are perfect already.

'Striving is a tool of the ego, to keep you busy and desperate whilst you are missing the point.

'Instead, the search for truth is a quiet and non-demonstrative business. It's not really a search or a business at all — but an unveiling. It is the fearless and simple exposing of error in ourselves, the ruthless unveiling of motive. And out of this quiet exposure arises a new space within us, in which we can receive new impressions.

'We begin to notice things. We begin to notice how we hurt people. We begin to become aware of the negativity that blights our days. We become aware of our endless self-justification. We become aware of the same life lived again and again and again.

'And as we notice, and refuse to avert our eyes, what essence we become. We are the bravest of the brave, and the most to be honoured, for the steady refusal to lie to ourselves or deceive ourselves, is perhaps the noblest human act of all.'

Simon Parke — *The Beautiful Life*

I hope that this quote resonates with the ideas of Erich Fromm quoted in Chapter 10 — Desire Leads Us. Given our position of acting from ignorance, we can at least infer some relative purpose, that is, contingent, localised, small-scale purposes that relate to our planet, our society, community or just to ourselves as individuals. In the absence of ultimate purpose, we can only come to some sort of balanced view of what might be legitimate and worthwhile purposes for our situation. Whilst recognising these to be necessarily parochial, they nevertheless allow us to devise a valuing of various actions and attitudes in relation to the human economy. It is this derivation of value based on real experience rather than idealism that is a key factor in the chapters that follow.

The desire to understand some kind of 'deeper' or 'higher' meaning to life in general and/or to our own lives in particular might well be a philosophical pursuit, independent of any emotional connotations we may bring. That said however, our mental constructs are for the most part 'after the event', that is, rationalisations of feelings and actions stemming from our emotions. It is not therefore necessarily so easy to distinguish between a purely philosophical quest and one that is really a personal one. Someone has said, there is only a need for meaning when there's a problem. We don't seem to feel the same need to find meaning in pleasure! If instead we focus on our real life as we experience it then meaning might be derived from our interactions rather than as an abstract and transcendent ideal.

If we accept that the universe appears to be pre-disposed towards nurturing life, then we at least have a beginning. We may call it providence, or perhaps grace. Again we do not know the real nature of this providence or grace.

If we are to deal with life though — as we all must — then part of this dealing will be to try to discern reasons and meanings, even whilst accepting that a full understanding will always be beyond us. We might look to truth, goodness and beauty as three aspects of being the means of grace. Truth — in terms of honesty in dealings between ourselves and others and equally and contiguous with this — in dealing with ourselves as individuals. Goodness — less in terms of moral respectability — and more in the sense of a genuine and heartfelt compassion and love for our fellow human beings and for the other creatures with whom we share this world. Finally, beauty — in its broadest context of living a wholesome life — at peace with ourselves, with others and with the world and engaged in creative work (which all work should be) and in creative play. Beauty — as we will see in the next chapter - undergirds all of this.

Whilst providence remains fundamentally mysterious, we can at least set this nurturing against the alternative of sheer indifference or hostility to life. Beyond this, as conscious beings, we can act on the world and to some extent we can understand and reflect upon the consequences of our actions. In this way, we can either enhance or frustrate the general disposition towards providence — we can be the means of grace, or the means by which grace is withheld. We might create meaning for ourselves then by being the means of grace in the world.

We are left however with a certain amount of 'middle ground' between a purely parochial understanding of meaning and something that is more over-arching — if not strictly speaking transcendent. There is meaning then of the parochial kind that refers simply to our intentions to carry out various acts or whatever in our lives - actions within the human economy. Then there is meaning that is a derivative of this, which acts as a guide and shapes communities and cultures. Over-arching meaning — albeit still parochial — is built up through *relationship* of various kinds.

The contention then is that it is through the quality of relationships that we make meaning for ourselves. As divided persons, we have a relationship with ourselves first and foremost, which is in a constant state of flux. How we deal with ourselves (with honesty, compassion and humour or with fear, anxiety and rationalism) is the starting point for meaning. Then with other people, further meanings open up. The self exists within the context of the human economy. Connections with others, which affirm the underlying reality of nonduality, thereby confer meaning to our lives. There might just be a chance meeting — the briefest of encounters with another. In that short space of time all of us have the opportunity to create meaning through kindness and generosity. Perhaps it is just a smile or a compliment and we move on. Alternatively, meaning can be confounded (or a different meaning created) by selfishness, anger or resentment. What if nothing else had any meaning apart from our interactions with others? I suspect the way many of us spend our time would be very different. Then there is our interaction with nature. This too is a relationship — one that we either deny or take delight in — or somewhere between these two. This nature includes our own bodily nature as well as the nature of the planet as a whole. Here we always meet a paradox. There is letting go and there is creativity, living and dying, form and formlessness. It is because all these things are really not separate — nondual — that they confound our human understanding. Nonetheless, the beauty of nature is the first source of awe, the cause of our celebration and the inspiration for being pleasure in the world.

Our own 'purpose' is of course circumscribed by the inevitability of our death. Ideas of leaving a 'legacy' are sooner or later realised to be vanity and our personal values are reconsidered in the light of this. A similar evaluation may be fruitful for humanity in general and the future of the planet. At the moment it seems that we want our species to endure forever — even if this entails the destruction of other species and possibly the need for finding new planets to inhabit. There is a certain amount of hubris in this to say the least! It seems to step up our parochial purpose to a universal one – to create some kind of eternal, unchanging kingdom for ourselves — heaven on Earth. Again it is the tendency towards transcendence rather than accepting the boundary of our human economy and indeed the boundary of our Earth's ecology. Could we ever come to the point where humanity as a whole would accept the inevitability that one day we will cease to be? If yes, then perhaps our idea of what would constitute legitimate purposes and values would re-align.

All of the above though still places us on shaky

ground. If we refer back to the quotation from Simon Parke, (and indeed the opening quote of this chapter) then we get the sense that even this derivation of meaning from relationships could still involve a degree of striving. It sounds like grace analysed and then packaged for general application. Can we step back from this somehow? As we go into our chapter on beauty, we will see there two effects. Beauty has the effect of helping us to see more beauty — to discover it in more ordinary things. Beauty also has the effect of letting us step aside from the world, to exist for a time in 'lateralness'. These effects in turn lead into seeking 'fairness' in terms of an equity and balancing in human relations — an equality that undergirds both justice and freedom. The starting point for all of this is then simply to see! If beauty remains unseen or unnoticed, then none of the virtuous consequences will follow. Two authors at least have taken up the simple notion of seeing as the key to life's meaning.

'The whole of life lies in the word "seeing".'

Pierre Tielhard de Chardin

'Other animals do not need a purpose in life. A contradiction to itself, the human animal cannot live without one. Can we not think of the aim of life as being simply to see?'

John Gray — *Straw Dogs*

We could summarise this chapter by saying that individual acts take on meaning as they manifest either loving attachment or alienating and disempowering violence. To the extent that we can be pleasure for others, we can find meaning in our lives. Stepping back though, the first act is to see! Seeing the beauty of the world leads us into this process of finding more beauty then creating beauty through being pleasure. This is contrasted with 'imposing' a meaning from some kind of transcendent knowledge, belief or revelation. It is a very awkward balance as there is an inevitable tendency in the human psyche to create meta-narratives on the one hand, or on the other hand to become dogmatic and idealistic about more parochial meanings. Stepping back, waiting, watching, unveiling our minds of delusions — these seem to be our best approaches to a universe that is fundamentally mysterious.

13. The Soul seeks Beauty first

'Beauty is the beginning of terror we can still just endure.'

Rainer Maria Rilke — Duino Elegies

'It is only as an aesthetic phenomenon that existence and the world are eternally justified.'

Friedrich Nietzsche

The word 'aesthetics' was invented by German philosopher, Alexander Gottlieb Baumgarten. He wrote: 'The end of Aesthetics is the perfection of sensuous knowledge.' At once we have the link between pleasure and beauty. This is further discussed by Alexander Lowen:

'...the body has feeling and it alone can experience pleasure, joy and ecstasy. It alone has beauty and grace, for apart from the body these terms are meaningless. Try to define beauty without referring to the body and you will see how impossible it is.'

Alexander Lowen — *Pleasure*

Beauty and the experience of beauty are not purely subjective. Beauty is part of the mystery that makes up the larger part of reality. It can therefore never be explained fully, or indeed explained away. We are not simply passive spectators — far less consumers — of beauty. We are part of the beauty of the world. Marsilio Ficino defined love as 'the desire for beauty' whilst Stendhal says, 'beauty is the promise of happiness.' Gandhi described his motivation as creating beauty. 'Real beauty is my aim,' he said. Richard Jefferies says this:

'The hours when the mind is absorbed by beauty are the only hours when we are truly alive.'

Whilst poet Robinson Jeffres says:

'... Integrity is wholeness,
the greatest beauty is
Organic wholeness, the wholeness of life and things,
the divine beauty of the universe.

It is important to distinguish between the word beauty and words like attractive that we sometimes use when describing another person. Attractiveness is in a way a commodification of beauty. Whilst the word beauty can be used in the context of simply describing a person's physical appearance it also carries with it at least some connotation of a more general 'rightness'. This is not necessarily to equate it with moral rightness, but it is certainly a wider affirmation of aesthetics. The word beauty leads us into a broad aesthetic that describes a right way of living — the 'good life'.

There is a sense in which a beautiful object or experience is not an enclosed sentiment. There is the possibility of danger, unpredictability and chaos lurking on the boundaries of the object or experience of beauty and this seems to accord much more with the experience of life. Beauty can drive us too far. An obsession with a particular aspect of beauty can lead to destructiveness and violence. Whilst it is beauty that inspires us toward creativity, that creativity can it seems also be destructive. Then of course it ceases to be creativity at all, but becomes violence. Beauty can drive us crazy; but there's good crazy and there's bad!

In the Arts, as we have noted, the sensuous has become suspect in Western culture. Thomas Berry addresses this point here:

'The world of mechanism has alienated us from the wild beauty of the world about us. Such is the power of art, however, that it can endow even the trivialities and the mechanisms of our world with a pseudomystical fascination. Supposedly this enables our world to avoid the epithet of being caught in an imitative Classicism or in a faded Romanticism. The result is to challenge any traditional norms of beauty by reversion to the wild simply through undisciplined turbulence, at times with an elaborate presentation of the trivial, or even what is referred to as a personal statement.'

Thomas Berry — *The Great Work*

As well as being reflective of wild nature and the beauty found therein, Art may also serve the function of bringing harmony, and indeed love. Take this quote from Nicholas Gogol:

'Art is the introduction of order and harmony into the soul, not trouble and disorder…If an artist does not accomplish the miracle of transforming the soul into an attitude of love and forgiveness, then his art is only ephemeral passion.'

Simon Parke (*The Beautiful Life*) says: 'Art, religion and philosophy should create a longing for home. The artist/priest/philosopher should bring this longing painfully to the surface.'

A longing for home, a longing for pleasure, are key features of our economy of descendancy, the place of the soul. Alexander Lowen contrasts this with our culture's longing for power:

'Despite this interest in beauty, the world grows uglier all the time. I believe this is because beauty has become an adornment rather than a virtue, an ego symbol rather than a way of life. We are committed to power not pleasure, as a way of life, and as a result beauty has lost its true meaning as an *image of pleasure*.'

> Alexander Lowen — *Pleasure* (My emphasis).

From Lowen then, and dating back to the ancient Greeks, we have beauty as an image of pleasure. For Plato, beauty was the idea (form) above all other ideas. The contrast between sign and symbol is especially important here. Beauty is image in the form of symbol — and as symbol, able to inspire rather than be prescriptive or limiting. Let's unpack this. We may set up an 'object of beauty', a sign, such as how we wish the world to be. In this sense, beauty can be similar to a spiritual quest, or to idealism in morality or politics. But the image then becomes something that we try to *own*. It is better for beauty to be a symbol in the sense that it can be something that we just *become*, such that we reflect the beauty that we find in the world. We then reflect our enchantment and engagement with life. Alfred North Whitehead gives a sense of this in his *Adventures in Ideas*. He says: 'The teleology of the universe is directed to the production of beauty... The type of truth required for the final stretch of beauty is a discovery and not a recapitulation.... Apart from beauty truth is neither good, nor bad... truth matters because of beauty.'

Friedrich Schelling puts it even more succinctly:

'The theoretical intelligence merely contemplates the world, and the practical intelligence merely orders it; but the aesthetic intelligence *creates* the world.'

Although this appreciation of beauty perhaps comes from the unknowable aspect of the universe, it seems to me that there is still part of us that understands and is changed by the experience of beauty. I think that this apprehension of beauty is a bigger clue to what life is about than either goodness or truth. Beauty — which seems the least definable of values — also seems the most real. Beauty speaks to the soul, both as its inspiration and as its goal. Beauty is something *given to us* first of all, and this sets it apart from other values.

As we've seen in the previous chapter, there is

another side to beauty that is less about aesthetics and more about seeing others in their personhood and in their humanity. Perhaps inevitably that connection reaches us at a deep emotional level. It is a step change from superficial prettiness or attractiveness to a profound beauty. It resonates with the awe that we feel in contemplating the universe as a whole.

Beauty then is not simply concerned with the arts or aesthetics or with attractiveness of physical appearance. Whilst emanating from mystery, it is nevertheless within the province of everyone to make beauty manifest in the world. Beauty inspires beauty — it inspires us to creativity. This can be in such things as our response to nature, care of others, friendships or good business practice. All these things, both simple and profound, can be gifts to the world. We are touching the void of mystery when we seek to bring beauty into the world. It is a means of grace, a pragmatic rather than an abstract spirituality. Making grace manifest in the world is a beautiful act.

A further paradoxical aspect to beauty is that beauty and imperfection go together. Otto Rank describes the quest for perfection as fundamentally an ego quest rather than a genuine spiritual quest. The search for beauty however, and discovering beauty in the midst of imperfection, is ultimately a quest which will transcend ego. It cannot be differentiated from a quest for the highest good. Richard Jefferies says: 'He who has got the sense of beauty in his eye can find it in things as they really are.' So, even in the imperfections of our world, beauty can be found. Even in the humdrum practicalities of an ordinary life, beauty can be brought forth and creativity can be inspired. Thomas Hardy says:

'The business of the novelist is to show the sorryness underlying the grandest of things and the grandeur underlying the sorriest of things.'

In similar vein, 'We ordinary people...' says Kenji Miyazawe, '...must forge our own beauty. We must set fire to the greyness of our labour with the wit of our own lives... What is the essence of this art of living? Of course, even this art should have beauty as its essence.'

Beauty is not something that we might respond to or might not. Beauty demands a response. Confucius was once asked to summarise his teachings in a simple manner and he did so with one word — reciprocity. Beauty — as in the beauty of the essence from which we have emerged, and the beauty of nature — requires a reciprocal response from us. Elaine Scarry addresses this point:

'Beauty seems to place requirements on us for attending to the aliveness ... of our world, and for entering into its protection.
'Beauty is, then, a compact, or a contract between the beautiful being (or person, or thing) and the perceiver. As the beautiful confers on the perceiver the gift of life, so the perceiver confers on the beautiful being the gift of life. Each "welcomes" the other.'

> Elaine Scarry — *On Beauty and Being Just*

The beauty and wildness of nature are likewise seeking a response from us. We ignore this at our peril. Psychologist James Hillman tells us that the ecological crisis is essentially an aesthetic problem. Humans however have a deep-rooted anger against nature for not being compliant to our wishes. We aspire to power over nature, but nature will not comply. Instead, she seeks our awe and our gratitude — and our humility. Our resistance — our lack of reciprocity — is having its consequences. In taming the wildness of nature outside ourselves, we have also tamed the inner wildness of our own souls. Creativity is thereby frustrated and trivialised. Reciprocity then is not an optional extra — in fact reciprocity *is* the soul's adventure in the world.

Often for those of us born into modern Western cultures, nature simply doesn't speak. Only those steeped in her language from birth will learn to hear her voice. Instead we are steeped in our own language of purely human signs — our letters and words, phones and the internet. All that is left is a dull vacancy, a sense of profound unease and guilt when we do occasionally stop to listen. Hearing nature and seeing beauty is a lifetime's work. This too takes grace and love.

Love sees beauty and responds to beauty with love. Plato said: 'Love's function is giving birth in beauty, both in body and in mind.' We have seen that to some extent this can be conflicted. Our relationship to wild nature and indeed to our own bodies is always somewhat unrequited. But we owe something back to beauty, to nature, to wildness! We must respond in kind by creating beauty in the world, both in terms of the physical things we make and also the relationships we form with other people, and with animals and plants and the environment. Keats may have said 'beauty is truth and truth beauty - that is all to know on earth and all ye need to know', (*Ode on a Grecian Urn*); but Aristotle saw instead a relationship between the beautiful and virtue, arguing that:-'Virtue aims at the beautiful.' The big link then is less between beauty and truth, more between beauty and goodness.

Beauty brings about a *radical 'de-centre-ing'* — takes us out of ourselves. This is a necessary process for bringing about good in the world. Another passage from Elaine Scarry takes up this thought and leads us into the further discussions of this work:

'...beautiful things give rise to the notion of distribution, to a life-saving reciprocity, to fairness not just in the sense of loveliness of aspect but in the sense of "a symmetry of everyone's relation to one another".
'It is clear that an *ethical fairness* which requires a "symmetry of everyone's relation" will be greatly assisted by an *aesthetic fairness* that creates in all participants a state of delight in their own lateralness [radical de-centring].'

> Elaine Scarry — *On Beauty and Being Just*

To summarise, the danger is that beauty is regarded just as an adornment, an aesthetic that is detached from anything such as rightness, harmony or love. Beauty then becomes mere attractiveness, as a commodity, that inspires only superficial pleasure at best, but at worst may be used as a means of power or destructiveness.

With beauty we have a connection with the wholeness of all things, the wildness of nature and the wildness within ourselves - our own bodies and souls. The wonder and awe that we feel as a result of beauty leads to gratitude and a creative response to the world. Beauty is the inspiration and creating beauty is the essential response — and with this, celebration, joy and compassion.

14. Start with Awe

'When we awaken awe, we awaken gratitude'

Matthew Fox

'Forfeit your sense of awe … and the Universe becomes a marketplace for you.'

Rabbi Herschel

We have grown used to the idea of an inert, value-free version of the physical universe, built from the ground up with blind force and a few varieties of elementary particles. But our lives are lived in direct opposition to this view. Our experience of the world is a highly subjective one and very much defined by value. Life as it is lived is all about choosing and valuing. How very different things look if we think that the universe has said 'yes' to life — as a choice and not just as an accident. I think that this makes the universe always on the 'half-full' side of things, weighted to the positive. It is not the bland, valueless, morally neutral, entropy-burdened and indifferent place sometimes portrayed to us, with consciousness perceived as a mere by-product of matter.

'What is the human?', asks Brian Swimme, 'The human is a space, an opening, where the universe celebrates its existence.' Elsewhere Swimme links our response to the universe with the flow and counterflow of form and formlessness. He says:

'...the ground of being is *generosity*. The ultimate source of all that is, the support and well of being is ultimate Generosity. All being comes forth and shines, glitters and glistens, because the root reality of the universe is generosity of being. That's *why* the ground of being is empty: every*thing* has been given over to the universe; all existence has been poured forth; all being has gushed forth because ultimate Generosity retains no thing.'

> Both quotes from Brian Swimme — *The Universe is a Green Dragon*

Likewise, deep ecologist writer Joanna Macey says that our starting point in relating to the universe should be gratitude whilst Meister Eckhart suggests that if the only prayer you say in your whole life is 'thank you' this will suffice.

In Indian philosophy it is said that Brahman is manifest as '*Sat-Chit-Ananda*' meaning, 'conscious joyful existence'. In similar vein, the Hindus describe Creation as '*Lila*' — God's play. The Earth has given us life. She provides our food and everything else we rely on for our continued existence. Perhaps you could stretch this and call it providence — or grace. Somehow life exists and thrives despite all the odds stacked against it. Somehow too, there is a strength that seems to come from beyond ourselves. The origin of grace is mystery. No matter how sophisticated our philosophy or theology might be, we are left in awe at the generosity and celebration of the universe. However, I believe that we can try to be the means of grace in the world — to make it manifest in our everyday lives. This would be a true and pragmatic form of spirituality – not abstract and other-worldly, but rooted in the here and now. Pleasure, beauty, awe, gratitude, creativity, celebration — they are all connected — feeding and nurturing each other as we enter them more deeply. A large part of the awe we feel for the world is derived from beauty. The beauty of nature has a special significance for us as our story unfolds. Originally it was the 'second book' in the Christian tradition, the manifest presence of God. Our modern Western culture has lost sight of this, so our relationship with beauty can be a conflicted one. Even so, as I hope we will see, our response to nature in awe is critical.

TWENTY-ONE LEVELS OF SELF-DECEPTION

15. Celebrate Life

'The universe, it could be said, exists to celebrate itself and revel in its own beauty.'

Gary Kowalski

I remember hearing a comedian contrasting the Brazilian carnival with the British equivalent — Shrove Tuesday and pancakes! The comedian commented by saying that perhaps we get the carnival we deserve! Western culture certainly has an odd way of relating to celebration. A bit like voting, it seems like it is relegated to a few special occasions. There's an orgy of materialism at Christmas, a couple of weeks of sunshine over summer, plus a few other breaks here and there. Holidays, feasts and parties are fitted around work and other responsibilities. The holidays and celebrations themselves are an ambiguous affair for some. Without the distractions of work, people find themselves confronted with relating to family who perhaps they only spend brief moments relating to the rest of the year. Even more difficult for some — we are confronted by ourselves, by the reality of who we are or might be.

Walking through the streets of any town or city on a Friday or Saturday night in the UK does however suggest that there is a lot of celebrating going on! The intention of revellers is perhaps simply to forget the problems of work and life generally and to find a few hours of fun. It is easy to be dismissive of this as somehow just excess of alcohol, but maybe we should not be so quick to judge.

There is a great need for celebration in all aspects of life — from daily meals through school and work, to spirituality. Why is school not more fun? Why is work usually just about getting things done with the least effort and cost? Why can we not spend more time finding ways to be creative in work and turning that creativity into celebration? Or, if that is too big a stretch, why not at least find more time for relaxing and socialising with our colleagues? Our culture does not relate well to its Christian festivals of Christmas and Easter. The heavy interpretations put upon these celebrations by evangelical Christianity makes them difficult symbols for a largely secular society to relate to. Is there any way forward from this? Perhaps we could bring back the very long association of festivals with the seasons? Reminders of our connection to the Earth and our reliance on Earth's providence might be more helpful than reminders of sin.

The money we are supposed to use to buy happiness — and presumably the chance for more play — never seems to arrive. Even if we ever have enough money, somehow play and celebration just refuse to be bought. The winners of lottery tickets after a few months apparently return to the same level of happiness prior to their win. So it seems that if you don't know how to party now, money's not going to help you learn!

For all the liberation of the last century or so we are also still quite a prudish nation. There is a strange ambivalence between licence on the one hand and an embarrassment about the body and sex on the other. The British seem to be strangely fascinated and yet disapproving of other people's nudity. We have high rates of teenage pregnancy. Somehow we just cannot get over our guilty fascination and so we just communicate our ambivalent hang-ups to the next generation. Why do we not celebrate our own bodies? Instead, we are presented with (or present ourselves with) images of what we 'ought' to look like and are left with the dilemma of what to do.

Society has turned play into a strangely serious enterprise. Sport has become big business. It is discussed as part of news programmes with at least equal seriousness as major world events. One imagines that if a reporter were to dare to say: 'Its only a game' they would not last long in their job! Even amateur involvement in sports is not often that playful. By contrast, if we watch young children at play, or think back to our own childhood then of course there is total absorption in the moment. Cares are forgotten and a child is completely unselfconscious in their imagination and enactment of games and stories. (Perhaps this is partly what is referred to when we talk of the ecstasy that adults have apparently lost.) If you are fortunate enough to have a young child of your own, then perhaps (hopefully) you have had the chance to lose yourself with them by engaging in their play. Or perhaps the children of friends afford this opportunity. There comes a point of course where this is lost — or at least set aside — for more 'grown-up' activities and concerns. Some adults though, never seem to be able to go back. They fear looking silly or being considered strange if they indulge in 'childish' behaviour. People's reactions to opportunities for playful behaviour say a lot about them. If you haven't played for a while, maybe it's time to give it a try! Eloi Leclere tells us that for Saint Frances of Assisi, salvation meant 'enchanted existence', whilst Meister Eckhart speaks of 'living without a why.'

Perhaps there is something else, a bit more subtle, that is going on. It seems sometimes that our culture is very mundane — not given to much flamboyance, exuberance or public displays of emotion. Occasionally however, there occur strange outpourings of celebration or grief that appear incongruous with the pervading culture. There seems to be an element of this in the binge drinking culture discussed above. Our need for celebration is being frustrated and is driving us to neurotic behaviour.

Matthew Fox addresses this in his work *Original Blessing*. He says:

'Another sin of omission...is the sin of limiting, always guarding or policing, pleasure. This sin of omitting Eros or love of life from our lives expresses itself in a preference for Thanatos, love of death. Thanatos represents the preoccupation with death, with the putting off of death, or with clinging to death-filled objects.

By sinning in this way we refuse to fall in love with life, to love what is loveable, to savour life's non-elitist pleasure, to celebrate the blessings of life, to return thanks for such blessings by still more blessing...

'The sin of consumerism is a child of the sin of emission of Eros. When religion fails to celebrate authentic Eros in our lives, we fall in love with ersatz pleasures which are subject/object pleasures which can be bought and sold but do not satisfy.'

The mention of Eros and Thanatos in this quote takes us back to the quote from Ken Wilber in a previous chapter. I've equated pleasure more with soul than spirit in this work, but of course there is spirit in celebration. Eros unbounded though takes us back to the economy of ascendancy and it is important not to muddle the fulfilment of ecstasy as primarily a search for sensuality. Charles Taylor comments on this in his *Sources of the Self*:

'...sensuality was given a new value. Sensual fulfilment ... seems to be one of the irreversible changes brought about by the radical Enlightenment. The promotion of ordinary life, already transposed by deists into an affirmation of the pursuit of happiness, now begins to turn into an exaltation of the sensual. Sensualism was what made the Enlightenment naturalism radical.'

In a similar vein, according to Foucault, freedom without limits is no freedom at all.

From this, we can contrast celebration as an 'aim' — which is really just pleasure-seeking —

with a deeper sense of what it means to celebrate. This is something akin to the contrast made between beauty of a superficial kind as compared to beauty that speaks of a deep 'rightness' within people, creatures or things. Like beauty and morality, celebration can easily be made into a thing to which we then aspire; a commodity that we might acquire. How can we, by contrast, be the celebration of the world? It is clearly linked to Brian Swimme's 'being pleasure for others' and in finding delight in all things.

We are in a process of becoming, but also we have already become (when looked at from the 'view from eternity' - to use Spinoza's phrase). We are already all that we ever need to be! (Even Grace Jantzen, whose work was examined in some detail earlier, has an element of becoming — of process — in her work. Just be!) So, start by celebrating yourself! Imperfect, precarious, frail, vulnerable, confused, or all of the above. All of this is telling us that we do not need to aspire — either in the world of work, or relationships or religion or spirituality. We can just delight in our own being!

This way of looking at ourselves translates easily into caring about others. When we acknowledge and take delight in the true beauty of others (not just their superficial attractiveness) then this is compassion. It is a further reason for celebration.

So, celebration is essential for genuine compassion. Compassion is rescued from being dull moralising, or even from being mercy by combining celebration with justice. When our families and communities and the wider community of all of life run in harmony, then this is justice. Again, justice is an expression of beauty and a cause for celebration. Because all is one, we are not separate from others or from nature. Compassion for and celebration of ourselves cannot be separated from compassion and celebration of all.

Within the context of the human economy of course there are times when we will fail to do what we should do or to treat others as they deserve to be treated. There is a 'parochial' journey to be made if you like, in finding ways to accommodate ourselves to what the world can reasonably expect of us. There will always be ambiguity in this, as often the world needs to be more accommodating of difference. This is part of our frailty and vulnerability as humans. We are time-bound and rarely glimpse that view from eternity described in the preceding paragraphs. But we can at least learn to laugh at ourselves, even as we are caught up in this limited perspective!

We are only a moment away from hilarity! The difficulty with society and with ego is that they take themselves too seriously. Humour is a great way to take us from the economy of ascendancy back down into the economy of descendancy, where celebration rules.

16. Allow for Darkness, Chaos and Randomness

'The Ground of the soul is dark'

Meister Eckhart

'The inner being of a human being is a jungle. Sometimes wolves dominate, sometimes wild hogs. Be wary when you breathe! At one moment gentle, generous qualities, like Joseph's pass from one nature to another. The next moment vicious qualities move in hidden ways. A bear begins to dance. A goat kneels!'

Mevlana Jelaluddin Rumi

The soul is rooted in mystery. Darkness and chaos are as much part of who we are as light and beauty. The soul mediates between our essence and our personality to make us the person we are. We may be fortunate in that all these things conspire to allow the lighter side of our souls to shine through. Or it may be that darkness and chaos come to the fore. This does not make the soul itself evil — it is just that the acts committed by the darker side are called evil because they can hurt others. Evil therefore remains a moral problem — something to be contained and fled from — but the darkness and chaos from which evil is born are not evil in themselves. There is no need for a spiritual cure and no need for us to try to force change on our own souls.

If the true nature of the universe is mystery, hidden from us, then we must accept that any explanation of such matters is beyond our grasp. The feeling of this mystery is somehow bitter-sweet — will always be conflicted as it is the meeting point of form and the formless. There is darkness in every soul. We carry with us a sense of our own mortality and perhaps vestiges of our pre-conscious past. Craziness, darkness, fear, longing, pain — these things are part of every person. To wish them away is to deny part of ourselves. So, life and love will always be bitter-sweet, because life is balanced on a knife-edge.

What we so often seem to avoid doing is to *enter into* darkness and chaos. Any sign of stress or discomfort and our culture's reaction is to immediately seek some 'fix'. The fix is often reacting only to symptoms — anything to get us back to work — anything to return us to relative happiness and contentment. Why not instead dwell for a while in darkness? Why not withdraw from the world and spend some time in the shadows? Perhaps it is a luxury to be able to do this. But perhaps it is also our culture's poor response to these matters that makes this seem an odd suggestion.

On the pragmatic level, we are forced to accept the circumstances that are presented to us. This is easy enough when life is good. It is pain and sadness that are the problems. In one way or another religion tries to sweeten the pill of these things by offering explanations for their occurrence. Not only is pain and sadness accepted they might even be embraced. Mainstream Christianity feels the need to separate evil from the rest of creation. It denies evil a real existence in a way and claims that it will ultimately be defeated. Eastern religions would say that the distinction between what we regard as good or bad experiences is illusory. But it is so difficult not to see this as a rationalisation. What if there is no afterlife, no literal soul that is 'growing', 'learning' or 'experiencing'? Can pain and sorrow still be accepted in such a world?

At least the Eastern faiths acknowledge fully the reality of suffering! Acceptance is a useful and beneficial attitude towards life. Most of our lives involve events and circumstances that are beyond our control and often beyond our power to change. If we can simply learn to live with these things — honest about where we stand — then that is all to the good. Some Buddhist traditions speak of fully realising our existential situation. At the same time however, there may be opportunities for changing ourselves or our circumstances. Wisdom lies in being able to discern when this is appropriate and finding the proper means of bringing about the changes that may be desired. Very often 'the means' are more about letting go and letting the soul heal herself — letting go and letting be. The change is less about ourselves and more about a creative response to the beauty in others and the beauty in the world.

The other concern is with self-acceptance. If you are a person not burdened by some physical or emotional problem and have grown up in relatively untroubled circumstances then self-acceptance is perhaps not a problem. In fact, the problem might be a blindness to any faults rather than a struggle to overcome. Perhaps though, more people than we are often aware of harbour issues that give them grief. Again, as with external circumstances, there is a balance to be sought between what can reasonably be accepted and what perhaps needs to change for the benefit of ourselves and those around us. Trying to change ourselves is never going to be easy. In fact, the effort itself can be self-defeating.

In an earlier chapter we looked at psychologist Erich Fromm's suggestions for self-analysis. We can repeat the importance of this process here. It may seem somewhat self-indulgent to look inward at our own concerns, when there may be a great deal of need all around us. But, as Simon Parke reminds us in *A Beautiful Life*: 'We hurt other by our unexamined suffering'. The real reasons for the way we react to other people and to circumstances are therefore deeply rooted in our own concerns. So the process of unravelling this is not wasted.

As Fromm suggests, it is often best simply to watch how we respond to things and circumstances — always trying to create space between what happens out in the world and our response to it in terms of emotions, speech and actions. We most of us live in our minds — anticipating future events and reflecting on past ones. If this process is a negative one — that is if we fear for the future and regret the past — then we will continually give ourselves the emotional hit that such imagined events incur. Stepping back from this and realising that the past is gone and the future could turn out (and probably will turn out) differently from how we expect is going to be a good strategy. To live always in the present moment can be very worthwhile. However, it is not given to many of us to find this practice easy. The imagination allows us to respond creatively to the world and can embrace both the past and the future in more positive ways.

Sometimes, in a dark place, our strategy can only be to remember what is good about ourselves and to try to celebrate our own being. It is good then to remember that we are already all that we ever need to be. But what if there are things that we find ourselves doing that are just not accepted by the society around us? What if we have some dark obsession or overwhelming compulsion to hurt others or to behave in ways generally rejected by society? What then? The need to change is clearly there, but we have already suggested that change might not be possible. The inner person, the essence or soul of a person remains unchanged, indeed remains perfect. But that means beauty and perfection are veiled by layers of damaged personality, rooted deep perhaps in childhood experiences, emotional pain, anger, bitterness, hate and ultimately self-loathing. I've suggested above that our human view of 'evil' is a moral one, but we might struggle to come to terms with a view of the soul as 'perfect' when it contains such darkness. I don't pretend to offer an answer to this — if indeed an answer could be offered. All that can be said is that such a person needs to be embraced rather than shut out. I beg you — where possible — to include and always to accept others who betray signs of such darkness. As we've seen, darkness runs through all of us. By excluding we cut off part of ourselves. By including, we heal.

The economy of descendancy has told us that we are part of our soul rather than our soul being part of us (even if we interpret this in a non-literal fashion). So too, our soul does not belong to us but has her own ways. She is part of mystery, with far more knowledge than we will ever find by ourselves.

If then the reality of who we are lies beyond what we can ever know, there is a sense in which trying to change is contradictory. If time is a mental construct and not the underlying reality, then there cannot be a 'future me' who is different from the current me. I am already all that I am going to be – or all that I ever need to be. When we speak of change then, it can only ever be meant in a parochial sense. It is hopefully of benefit to remember that we are all of us already far more than we could ever realise. Our efforts need to be made in the light of this.

17. Beware Ideals

'This word is a hidden word and comes in the darkness of the night. To enter this darkness put away all voices and sounds all images and likenesses. For an image has never reached into the soul's foundation where God herself with her own being is effective.'

Meister Eckhart

'All that was once directly lived has become mere representation.'

Guy Debord — Society of the Spectacle

Compassion, freedom, equality, justice and love are all ideals. They are useful and inspiring as images, as all images can be inspiring. However, we need to remember that these ideals are only realised in particulars. Treating ideals as aspirational risks them becoming ideology rather than a living reality. This thought is well expressed by Erich Fromm in his book, *The Art of Being*:

'It is striving that is rooted in the ambiguity of man's existence and that has the aim of finding an answer to the uncertainty of life by transforming a person, an institution, an idea into an absolute, i.e., into an idol by the submission to which the illusion of certainty is created. It is hardly possible to overestimate the psychological and social significance of idolatry in the course of history, that great illusion that hobbles activity and independence.'

Ideals will always stand outside the real world - that is their essential nature. We need to recognise this, embracing ideals, whilst understanding that they are only images of what might be. Ideals then can easily become idolatry or idealism. Ideology deduces reality, or makes sense of the world, via representations rather than directly. Grand notions of compassion, freedom, equality, justice and love are ultimately useless then unless they can cope with the mundane, workaday concerns of real lives. To miss this is to succumb to a patronising and pious dead end. It is maintaining a conversation, an interaction with ourselves, our communities and ultimately with all of nature that prevents ideals from becoming ideology. Hence hospitality — or conviviality — is a good way of seeing the outworking of compassion and fairness in society. Love is affectionate kindness as well as passion. (Again our 'economy of ascendancy' and 'economy of descendancy' are useful here. Love in particular is portrayed in heroic, aspirational terms by both religion and society at large. It is ascendant, spirit-led, erotic. It is all passion — whether that is the passion of God for humanity or the passion of young lovers. The economy of descendancy can seek to make love manifest in the particulars of everyday life. Eros tempered by Agapé.)

It is difficult to escape from idealism though and to find ways of grounding ideals in real life and real relationships. Much of the rest of this work takes up this concern. One ideal we will consider is that of intrinsic value. Beyond that, we can conclude that being the means of grace is the practice of making ideals manifest in the world — of making an economy of grace.

18. Intrinsic Value

'The universe is a communion of subjects, not a collection of objects.'

Thomas Berry

Western culture has been tracking towards the idea that value is purely subjective. Somehow, as long as there is consensus it is okay to redefine value in terms of what might serve some abstract ideal. Value therefore often ends up being commodified - in other words it is extrinsic rather than intrinsic.

We have thus far looked at compassion, freedom, equality, justice and love in the very broadest sense as ideals. All of these really have an underlying assumption. That assumption is that the subjects of our compassion and so on are worthy to receive our gift. The assumption is that others and myself have some value over and above mere usefulness. That is, people (and also animals and plants) have intrinsic value as distinct from extrinsic value or mere commodity.

You might say that this value is an assumed goodness to all of life. Along with truth and beauty, the goodness is rooted in mystery. It is beyond explanation, but it is the reason for our celebration of life. It is the motivation for our compassion. Compassion in turn expresses itself in seeking justice and freedom where these are needed. All in all, the intrinsic value of ourselves allows us to celebrate ourselves. We are all that we ever need to be and it is always enough. And the intrinsic value of others allows us to respond to their beauty with spontaneous creativity. It inspires us to give pleasure to others. To be pleasure for them.

The essence that is our true selves can never be anything other than perfect. So, this is the ultimate source of intrinsic value. Only in the manifest world can any kind of contingency arise. Darkness and chaos, as we have seen, may manifest in destructive and evil acts within the human economy. We could say that the response to beauty here has failed. Beauty is too much and for some reason the destructive personality flees from it or crushes it rather than trying to reflect it back into the world. But this is not ultimate reality. Even the most depraved and debased person is not pure evil. They still have intrinsic value. To deny this is to deny the true reality of the world. It is also to deny a part of ourselves. We are all one, so there is darkness and chaos running through us all.

The assumption of intrinsic value then is the basis for all our action in the world. We might more generally just call it our response to beauty as beauty is the supreme value from which all other values are derived. Correct valuing — a creative response to beauty — is the currency of our economy of grace. The creativity comes from beyond ourselves - it is grace made manifest in the world through us.

19. Derive Ethics from Relationships

'Compassion is the working out of our interconnectedness; it is the praxis of interconnectedness.'

Hildegard of Bingen

Compassion is often now taken to simply mean mercy — and mercy is something of a sentimental thing. It can be a condescension to people in need, which whilst sometimes very welcome, nonetheless maintains the 'power over' dynamic that is so insidious in our culture. In this work, put simply, compassion is taken to mean justice and celebration, and this is in relation to the oneness of all life.

Because of its aspiration to transcendence, spirituality tends to view compassion, justice and love as ideals. They are seen as timeless qualities that exist outside the realm of human interaction and which we simply appropriate or fail to appropriate. Almost unwittingly, metaphysics becomes the primary concern. Instead of: 'How should we live?' — the first question becomes: 'What is the world like?' What is compassion as an ideal — in the abstract? The result is that truth, knowledge and belief far outweigh relationship in terms of trying to become more compassionate and to act more justly. It is suggested here and throughout this work that this is not a good approach. It is something that occurs because of a long-standing bias toward objectivity and abstract truth - particularly in Western culture. Erich Fromm contrasts the notion of being with that of becoming:

'... the idea that being implies change, ie. that being is *becoming*, has its two greatest and most uncompromising representatives at the beginning and at the zenith of western philosophy: in Heraclitus and in Hegel.
'The position that being is a permanent, timeless, and unchangeable substance and the opposite of becoming, as expressed by Parmenides, Plato, and the scholastic 'realists', makes sense only on the basis of the idealistic notion that thought (idea) is the ultimate reality. If the *idea* of love (in Plato's sense) is more real than the experience of loving, one can say that love as an idea is permanent and unchangeable. But when we start out with the reality of human beings existing, loving, hating, suffering, then there is no being that is not at the same time becoming and changing. Living structures can be only if they become; they can exist only if they change. Change and growth are inherent qualities of the life process.'

> Erich Fromm — *To Have or to Be?*
> (Author's emphases.)

This quote very much echoes Grace Jantzen's concept of 'natals' (as opposed to mortals) and her ideas on becoming expressed in her book 'Becoming Divine'. Looking at Emmanuel

Levinas' critique of morality in western philosophy, Jantzen comments:

'The disastrous consequences of such an onto-theological system in which knowledge is itself violence are only too apparent, not least in how ethics is conceived within such a framework. If ethics is held to follow from being... this effectively *subordinates ethics to ontology*. But this means ethics itself is founded in violence — that is, in the unethical.'

Jantzen goes on to quote directly from Levinas:

'To affirm the priority of *being* over *existents* is to already decide the essence of philosophy; it is to subordinate the relation with *someone* who is an existent, (the ethical relation) to a relation with the *being of existents*, which, impersonal, permits the apprehension, the domination of existents (a relationship of knowing), subordinates justice to freedom.'

The solution proposed by Levinas (and supported by Jantzen) is simply to know another person as a unique individual, in their 'radical otherness'. To treat others simply as examples of a universal or as members of a category is already to do violence to them. To treat others as individuals is to *celebrate their particular manifestation as embodied persons,* (or as Maurice Merleau-Ponty might describe us — 'body-subjects').

Levinas again:

'This is the question of meaning not being: not the ontology of the understanding of that extraordinary verb, but the ethics of its justice. The question *par excellence* of the question of philosophy. Not "why being rather than nothing?", but how being justifies itself.'

> All quotes from Grace Jantzen —
> *Becoming Divine*

It is important to stress though, as with the opening quote of this chapter, that we are already fully connected as embodied persons. The oneness of life makes this something we cannot avoid — even if we may want to sometimes! Also, when we set up right and wrong as absolutes, we turn them into something else. This ceases to be ethics in the sense of relationship and becomes instead a bureaucracy.

From an 'eternal' perspective our souls 'just are'. The idea of change is meaningless until some boundary is set within which a measure can be taken. Depending on the boundary, or the description or economy that we adopt, it could be said perhaps that the soul changes over the course of a human lifespan. Whether that change is for better or for worse again depends on how we set up our economy. If we choose to look at how the soul accommodates the life of her host to the particular mores and customs in which she finds herself, then we could perhaps stipulate an improvement or a decline. But from an eternal perspective, the soul is perfect.

The criticism of Western philosophy from Jantzen and others then is that truth is paramount! Value is only realisable through ideals, so morality is seen in terms of relating to something that is fixed and external. Even where morality is rejected, or considered to be 'relative' it is actually just a rebellion against this particular interpretation of what value really is. The underlying assumption is that of a fixed truth, and knowledge in terms of justified true belief is never questioned. This in turn means that value that arises from within the human economy, as an ongoing interaction between embodied persons, is disregarded. There is however one underlying truth that validates this notion and that is nonduality or interbeing, or simply the oneness of all things. As embodied persons, we are nonetheless already connected. We cannot choose to opt out of this and be value-free. All choices we make necessarily add to, or detract from, compassion.

To summarise then: I am just me — not good or bad in myself. However, I am also a person set within a context - some kind of human culture or community. It is in that context that I might be viewed as either good or bad and my individual

acts can be judged to be one or the other. (It is in this context that 'becoming' over 'being' takes on its true significance.) There is always a balance to be struck between how much accommodation I am willing or able to make. Likewise, in dealing with others, there is a sense in which the real person stands outside any judgement of goodness or badness. Within the context of the human economy however, we can assign a measure of responsibility to act rightly and a measure of blame if the values of the human economy fail to be upheld. Within the economy of grace, we step back from this and see the person just as a person — beautiful in essence aside from any right or wrong. Deserving always our compassionate response. This is surely our toughest decision. For if the soul is perfect and the character of a person is all that it ever needs to be, then at what point does evil enter into the equation? Is it nothing more that a particular culture's interpretation of right and wrong? This is the question often posed of religion — how could a good God allow evil? — but it is bringing it home to individuals. How can a perfect soul commit evil? The only alternative I can see is to accept the universe as random and then the problem of evil vanishes (although not, of course, evil itself). But with a random universe, in place of the question of evil there are the questions of where did all this complexity and order come from and how has consciousness come about? An intermediate position might be to say that consciousness has evolved with the universe and it must try to discern what is for the best just from the development of life. Then, souls are not perfect and individual character might not be all it could be and genuine evil becomes a distinct possibility. But the question of order — and where consciousness came from in the first place — still remains.

Those who have had a 'mountain-top experience' — seen the world as serene, inter-connected and beautiful in itself — along with the mystical tradition generally, are testifying to a universe that is perfect in itself. As such, I prefer to stay with this vision of the world as seen from the mountain-top. I accept evil as a reality but see it as an unexplained paradox from within our limited human view of things.

20. Compassion and Desire meet in Embodied Persons

'If you want others to be happy, practice compassion. If you want to be happy, practice compassion'

Dalai Lama

'Out beyond ideas of wrongdoing and rightdoing there is a field; I'll meet you there.'
Mevlana Jelaluddin Rumi

'Compassion is the antidote to the self-chosen poison of anger.'

Author unknown

How can I satisfy my desire? How can I have compassion for others? The idea expressed in this chapter is that these two questions, which were the starting point for the whole work, are really just the same question. If we look again at the meaning of compassion used in this work — as justice and celebration — then hopefully the reality of this will start to become clear. Compassion is much more than a response to the suffering of others in acts of mercy — it is also a response to the joy in others. Joy is found in relationship — either relationship with other embodied persons, or with nature. There is beauty in such interactions — indeed beauty is the highest aim as it embraces both compassion and love. Also, the idea of embodiment is critical. If we were only to relate as minds, then we would be back to the problems that we examined in the previous chapter. We would only have the idea of love rather than actual interaction. We are so caught up in this representation of experience, that the reality of embodiment, the actual experience of joy, gets immediately translated into a thought process. As such, it enters the ever-receding horizon of signifiers that our language has constructed and it is lost. It is so difficult, almost impossibly difficult, for us to grasp the reality of this crucial difference between being totally at one with our actions and representing our actions as examples in reference to an external truth. Eastern thought however, has long since understood this point. The passage below from the Tao will seem obscure from our Western perspective, but illustrates very well the way in which we lose ourselves when we try to quantify action:

'The person of superior integrity takes no action,
Nor has he a purpose for acting.
The person of superior humaneness takes action,
But has no purpose for acting.
The person of superior righteousness takes action,
And has a purpose for acting.
The person of superior etiquette takes action,
But others do not respond to him;
Whereupon he rolls up his sleeves
And coerces them.

Therefore, when the Way is lost,
Afterwards comes integrity.
When integrity is lost,
Afterwards comes humaneness.
When humaneness is lost,
Afterwards comes righteousness.
When righteousness is lost,
Afterwards comes etiquette.

> *Tao te Ching* (as translated by Victor H. Mair).

There is no thought here to having a 'morality' or a code of ethics. From within the Way there is no need. We are reminded that all explanations are just human constructs and therefore cannot reach any kind of explanation of reality — a theme of which we are best to remind ourselves constantly. The person of integrity doesn't necessarily do nothing. This person however recognises that all action outside of the Way is a human construct and therefore is second best. Acting from within the Way cannot be defined, although potentially it could be lived. All responses separate action from being. But we are not separate from our action or inaction — we are our action in the world. In the previous chapter, we saw how Western culture has subordinated ethics to ontology, or morality to truth — in Grace Jantzen's words — being (in the sense of embodying value) over existence. Jantzen goes on to look at how Levinas understands desire in terms of a response to the face of others — to their embodiment:

'In Levinas' thinking, desire itself is reshaped by the face of the other, shaped into a response that goes far beyond myself. It is not the name of a lack, but the release from self-enclosure, a joy therefore, that is always in excess, and a desire that is not diminished in its fulfilment. In all this, it bears the trace of the divine...

'Such excessive desire, such interminable yearning and fulfilment, is not, for Levinas, something which is strictly 'spiritual'.... On the contrary, since it is a response to the face of the neighbour or stranger, and concerned with the needs they express, *desire is embodied*. Embodiment, for Levinas ... *is the very site of transcendence.*

'*"The human subject is first of all an animated and inspired body*, the incarnate, affective spirituality of a passion for the other.... Transcendence is no longer an ascent to a heaven of the ideal or the sublime, but humble endurance of everyday life, touched, affected, wounded, obsessed and exhausted. *A human subject is an inspired body.*'"

> (Jantzen quotes from Adriaan Theodoor Peperzak. Emphases mine.)

We have traced the outworking of these ideas through several chapters now. Our starting point has been simply to see. In seeing, we see the more obvious beauty in the world, both in nature and in other people. This beauty inspires awe and gratitude. It welcomes us and leads us into finding more beauty. It allows us to step outside of ourselves — to take an eternal perspective. It helps us to let go of those things that we cling to at our cost — both physical things (materialism) and emotional and psychological things. In letting go, we are free to create. What we create is more beauty in the world. We become pleasure — pleasure for ourselves and pleasure for others. Beauty also manifests as a fairness in our dealings with the world. Equality is the starting point for both justice and freedom. As justice and freedom are brought about, we celebrate with others in joy. This is our compassion, this is fulfilment of desire. The emphasis on pleasure, celebration and joy and their strong links to compassion, equality, freedom and justice might be regarded with suspicion by some. It is not the usual moral tone! Alexander Lowen stresses the need for a balance:

'Talking of love, but disassociating it from its relation to pleasure is moralising. Morality has never solved the emotional difficulties of man. On the other hand, stressing the importance of pleasure in disregard of the basic need of people for some security, stability and order in their lives is irresponsible. This can only lead to chaos and misery. The human condition needs a *creative* approach to its opposing needs. *We must recognise that the more pleasure one has, the more one's ability to love. We must know that in offering our love, we increase our pleasure.'*

> Alexander Lowen — *Pleasure* (my emphases).

This link between compassion for oneself and compassion for others is a deep and important one:

'By dropping or letting go of worlds of subjects/objects, we sink into a consciousness of interdependence and indeed of transparency. Our experiences of transparency and synchronicity are experiences of no-thing-ness, and vice versa. As we allow this truth to penetrate us more and more deeply we begin to realise the truth of compassion: to relieve another person's pain or to celebrate another's joy is to relieve one's own pain and to celebrate one's own joy.'

Matthew Fox — *Original Blessing*

A similar idea is expressed by Thomas Merton:

'The whole idea of compassion is based on a keen awareness of the interdependence of all these living beings, which are all part of one another and are all involved with one another.'

Thomas Merton — *Marxism and Monastic Perspectives*

Returning us to our widest perspective, a simple quote from Ken Wilber reminds of the link between compassion and oneness:

'...the Many returning to and embracing the One is Good and is known as wisdom; the One returning to and embracing the Many is goodness, and is known as compassion.'

Ken Wilber — *Sex, Ecology. Spirituality*

Finally, and leading us into the next chapter, a passage from Danah Zohar:

'In my own being, which draws its very existence from the creation of relational wholes, I am by nature a creature which is stuff of the same substance with love, truth and beauty.

Not because I create them, but because the nature of my own consciousness is synonymous with the nature of their meaning. Through my own being, I have the capacity *to act as midwife to their expression in this world*, and they in turn mould and make the self that I am. The same would be said of all spiritual values, all of which share the common quality that they create relationship, and thus are stuff of the same substance as myself. There is a firm basis for commitment to them.'

> Danah Zohar — *The Quantum Self* (my emphasis).

21. Be the Means of Grace

'If you want to get across an idea, wrap it up in a person.'

Ralph J. Bunche

Participation is called 'at-one-ment' by D.H. Lawrence and called grace by theologians. Set against this, the word for devil in Hebrew — *Shatan* — literally means 'no response'.

We have used the terms 'nonduality' and 'mystery' to refer to the place from which the manifest world has sprung. It is non-essence and formlessness but from formlessness form has emerged. These terms carry no implication of intentionality — no ultimate purpose is presumed. The word 'grace' takes things a little further. The word carries an implication of benevolence. Grace is a reality, not because it is somehow given to us from outside the world but because we are grace. We are beauty, awe, gratitude, celebration, pleasure, joy, compassion, equality, freedom, justice, love. Likewise, if the universe is '*Lila*' — that is, God's joy — then value is inherent in the universe. Reality is somehow not neutral and yet the reason why this might be so is forever beyond our comprehension.

In the style adopted throughout this work, we have already named this process as the 'economy of grace'. What is the grace economy? The grace economy is about embodied persons in relationship. It is an economy about particular individuals and their particular circumstances, rather than a transcendent moral or idealistic code. Donna Haraway says this:

'We seek not the knowledge ruled by phallogocentrism (nostalgia for the presence of the one true Word) and disembodied vision, but *those ruled by partial sight and limited voice*. We do not seek partiality for its own sake, but for the sake of the connections and unexpected openings situated knowledge makes possible... the joining of partial views and halting voices into a collective subject position that promises a vision of a means of *ongoing finite achievement, of living within limits and contradictions, ie., of views from somewhere.'*

Donna Haraway (my emphases). (Haraway is contrasting with Thomas Nagel's 'view from nowhere', mentioned briefly in an earlier chapter, which is in many ways the epitome of the current world view.)

Sharon Welch compares 'beloved community' (the idea for which she has developed from Martin Luther King) with the Kingdom of God. She says:

'The Kingdom of God implies conquest, control and final victory over the elements of nature as well as over the structures of injustice. The 'beloved community' names the matrix within which life is celebrated, love is worshipped, and partial victories over injustice lay the ground work for further acts of criticism and courageous defiance.'

> Sharon Welch, as quoted by Grace Jantzen in *Becoming Divine*.

Welch continues:

'A 'symbolic' rather than an ethic or an ideal. Divinity is not a mark of that which is other than finite. *Grace is not that which comes from outside* to transform the conditions of finitude. Divinity, or grace, is the resilient, fragile, healing power of finitude itself. The terms *holy* and *divine* denote a quality of being within the web of life, a process of healing relationship, and they denote the quality of being worthy of honour, love, respect and affirmation.

> Sharon Welch, as quoted by Grace Jantzen in *Becoming Divine* (first emphasis mine, others are the author's).

Jantzen comments:

'...the divine that is encountered is immanent in the beauty, and pain and struggle of this world and our relationships in it.'

She goes on to suggest that in order for societies to be 'beloved' they must be 'performative' rather than simply intellectual. Individuals will '...perform deeds and narrative stories... as embodied suffering subjects.' All of this relates of course to Jantzen's defining us as 'natals' rather than mortals. Natals are significant because they are born — they are in a process of becoming. By contrast, mortals are only defined by the inevitability of their death. Strangely, despite our society's denial of death, we nonetheless continue with this term, perhaps because as observed in an earlier chapter, the consequence of unlimited 'spirit', our economy of ascendancy, is that genuine fulfilment is inevitably relegated to an abstract life after death. Whilst this was once only or mainly a religious conviction, it is now covertly embedded in our entire culture. For Western culture, things have a beginning (often out of nothing) and then an end. By contrast, as suggested by many of the authors in this work, life is better viewed as a process of becoming. The idea of narrative and performative acts is important too. It is the alternative symbolic, which takes us away from the purely abstract images, reflected in our language and so insidious in our culture and moves us instead toward an ethic that is a lived reality. The narrative of the beloved community — the grace and beauty of particular people and place — is the alternative symbolic.

In this work I have deliberately tried to avoid the word love, except as it sometimes occurs as one of our ideals, the images to which we are drawn as a concept, as described in earlier chapters. Love is a difficult word in our culture. Whilst our other ideals remain abstract goals — and this is the position very much being challenged in this work — love is particularly awkward because the meaning of the word itself is far from clear. We get a flavour of a different kind of loving above as Jantzen describes immanence in beauty, pain and struggle and says of the beloved community that it is made up of 'embodied suffering subjects'. Catherine Keller says: 'To love is to bear with the chaos'. A broader description of this point is given by Simon Parke:

'We will also be cautious about attaching ourselves to the word 'love' for the word has lost its way. Its origins are fine. Openness towards all is the spring from which love once flowed. But it has become polluted by the ego, and cut off from its source. From being an attitude to life that acknowledges all as equal, and lives the ultimate oneness of reality, blessing all and favouring no-one, it has become a high-voltage emotion, something possessive and jealous and therefore never far from hate.
'Openness has become a controlling and localised emotion called 'love'. Love is now shorthand for something untouched by wonder.'

Action in the world then can easily become an obsession of the ego. We have seen already that our quest for fulfilment of desire is potentially just another abstract goal or ideal to which we might aspire. A thing to possess rather than a living reality. Matthew Fox contrasts compassion with compulsion:

'This temptation to compulsion is one more reason why contemplation and solitude are so important an ingredient for compassion. We need to learn to let go even of our good intentions, our good works, and attitudes and this kind of letting go is learned in solitude and cosmic contemplation.'

Solitude and contemplation are therefore a

necessary counterpoint to our action in the world. They put us back in touch with the formlessness of which we spoke in Chapter 2. Grace and our notions of parochial purpose are then only background. Beauty too, as we explored in Chapter 13, can have the effect of taking us out of ourselves. The reality of what we do and why we do it is always going to be part of mystery. This in turn is touched on by Simon Parke as he speaks about the pursuit of truth:

'The pursuit of truth is not an intellectual affair. It is merely the dismantlement of our attitudes.
'To receive truth, I need above all things to create something new inside me, a space not previously developed. I need to create a middle space, or in-between place — somewhere that is other than both my starting essence and my claustrophobic personality. A place where I can take off my coat and simply experience myself. A place to listen to who I am, free from the tyranny of personal agendas. A place where I can begin to trust my experience as something other than my manipulative ego. A place where I could prepare to hear the truth and perhaps recognise it when I do. What a fine place that would be, if I could create it: an inner sanctuary, a clean space within.
'The search for truth is all in the preparation.'

Parke continues:

'This moment of discovery and revelation...has been called the mustard-seed moment. It is a moment requiring two simultaneous experiences; the external experience of the thing perceived, and the internal experience that is ready to appreciate it. That is why two people can look at the same view and experience very different reactions. They share the same external experience. But their internal experiences are poles apart.

'We see outside us what is inside us.'

Simon Parke also speaks of how mystery engages with the world via ourselves as persons:

'At the heart of the mystery is your essence. It rests wonderful and wild at the heart of your being, untouched by the savagery of life and indestructible against its onslaughts. It remains as it was at the beginning, perfect and unscarred, at the centre of your soul.

'Your soul is the adventure of your essence. It is through your soul that your essence engages with life.

'It is also through your soul that you lose your way.'

Grace is the normal English translation of Agapé. Grace is also defined as love in action. Eros and Agapé are often seen as being opposing nodes of love, but I hope it is now evident they can work together. Agapé is the basis of the 'beloved community' in which Eros can properly flourish. The alternative symbolic — ascendancy embraced by descendancy, spirit tempered and made wise by soul. The masculine brought back into correct relationship with the feminine.

We have seen how the fulfilment of desire may become another ideal to which we aspire — a compulsion of the ego rather than something genuinely lived. Grace is in danger of being this too if we treat it wrongly. Are we in danger of creating another ideal out of grace? What makes it different from any of the other abstract goals we have identified? We will return to these questions in the Conclusion, but for now this quote from Matthew Fox suggests that we are already grace and provides us with part of the answer:

'What is being said is that compassion — interdependence — already is the universe. We do not have to make it anew. Compassion, one might say, is a *grace* and not a *work*.

Matthew Fox — *Original Blessing*

Note that Fox says not that grace is *in* the universe, he says grace *is* the universe. There is something fundamentally different going on here. It is more about creating a space within myself to allow grace to flow, rather than my making grace, or being compassionate. We are the grace of the world. Unless we allow ourselves to be the means of grace, there is no grace. This is where the term 'panentheism' has its meaning. Grace resides in mystery. I can only create a space within myself to allow grace to flow. But — within the context of the human economy - *I am grace*. This is the 'economy of grace'. 'Wrap it up in a person' the opening quote of this chapter suggested; But the only people around to wrap grace up in is you and I.

Some final words from Brian Swimme sum up all that has been explored in this work:

'...we awake to fascination and we strive to

156

fascinate. We work to enchant others. We work to ignite life, to evoke presence, to enhance the unfolding of being. All of this is the actuality of love. We strive to fascinate so that we can bring forth what might otherwise disappear. But that is exactly what love does: Love *is* the activity of evoking being, enhancing life.'

He goes on:

'...do I desire to *become pleasure?*'
'...our own truest desire is *to be* and *to live*. We have ripened and matured when we realize that our deepest desire in erotic attractions is to become pleasure ... to enter ecstatically into pleasure so that giving and receiving pleasure become one simple activity. Our most mature hope is to become pleasure's source and pleasure's home simultaneously. So it is with all the allurements of life. We become beauty to ignite the beauty of others.'

TWENTY-ONE LEVELS OF SELF-DECEPTION

Conclusion

'Our greatest illusion is to believe that we are who we think ourselves to be.'

Henri Amiel

'There will come a time when you believe everything is finished. That will be the beginning.'

Louise L'Amour — Lonely on the Mountain

Eros and Agapé

Eros/Agapé is of course the main division of this work. We have seen that Eros is favoured in our culture and this is reflected in abstract and unachievable goals. Agapé, by contrast, is love looking to make connections with all that is around us. This side of life is very much neglected. Many of the boundaries, the economies, identified in this work have been reflections of this fundamental split. However, both are needed and both can be brought back into balance. Eros, we might say, is the adventure of the soul in the world, even although we have identified soul more with the Earth. But in this is the balance, the adventure lies much closer to home. Firstly, just in seeing. Seeing the fragile beauty in all things. Seeing the ordinary things in life transformed into the extraordinary. Then, responding. So, Eros, properly brought within the bounds of Agapé, is a welcome and essential part of us.

The Two Questions

We introduced two questions at the start of this work. The first concerned the satisfaction of my own desire. The second was about how I might rationalise that satisfaction or accommodate it with the needs of the wider world in which we live. We described the first question to be a central concern of psychoanalysis whilst the second is the concern of Marxism, or Socialism generally. We are now in a position to go back to these initial questions and summarise where the argument of this work has brought us.

Psychoanalysis associates with the individual, Marxism with collectives. Psychoanalysis is the way to attend to pleasure and Marxism the way to attend to needs. But psychoanalysis suggests that we have abdicated our ecstasy when just infants. Happiness is something we feel we must be constantly seeking, so that desire and ecstasy can be recovered.

The recovery of ecstasy is really just a myth. It might describe something of the playfulness and delight that can be achieved when we are able to forget ourselves for a while in pleasure — in particular when we greet the world with awe and recognise its fragile beauty. But more generally, the loss and recovery of ecstasy are just secular versions of the fall and redemption of Christianity. 'Recovery of ecstasy' is just an abstraction and places pleasure as always somehow beyond us. Why not instead the familiar animal pleasures of 'feeble flesh'? The occasional blue sky, sunshine, rest, companionship, idleness? Real life is made up of these haphazard pleasures - not a sterile eternal happiness of epic proportions.

The state of our soul and who we are in our essence are not things given to us to know. We inevitably have a delusion of who we are and sometimes this is greatly at odds with how others see us. The delusion may be harmless enough and it might actually make us 'better' people in terms of being good citizens and morally upright, but it is a delusion nonetheless. Or maybe the delusion we have of ourselves needs to be examined and called into question. We identified four aspects of self-analysis from Erich Fromm and noted that there is a lot that we would be best to let go of — if only to make ourselves happier, let alone being any use to others or to the world at large.

Seeing ourselves a little and letting go is the place to start — the means by which our essence finds its adventure in the world. It is not about trying; striving to do something that is not yet achieved. It is opening a space within ourselves that allows the grace already in the world to become manifest to others and to ourselves.

Simon Parke addresses this point:

'The world is not the problem...the world is quite perfect. It is the performers who are the problem, the activists who want to make external things better. They are not at home to themselves — but insist on trying to lead others home. This is why things stay the same. Solutions imposed from outside are not solutions. They bring change — but not transformation. *For you cannot promote transformation beyond the degree of internal transformation of yourself.'*

> Simon Parke — *The Beautiful Life* (my emphasis).

It is said by some that art and angels are the messengers between the unseen world and the world of phenomena. (The original meaning of the Greek *'daimon'* was as a messenger between the divine and human worlds.) Whether you choose to believe in angels, or agree with this function of art, the idea still stands that somehow mystery is communicated to us. If it were not so, there would be no becoming — indeed no world at all. Part of seeing is to see the 'angels' — those people we meet who communicate something from beyond themselves. It is the 'mustard seed moments' of which Simon Parke speaks. A truth is brought to us just at a time when we are ready to receive it. Likewise, for art. The artist, in helping us to see, opens us to new beauty, and then the cascading consequences of this where further beauty is perceived and creativity inspired. Perhaps the soul herself is a further messenger, from mystery to our consciousness. We look to Matthew Fox to summarise this section for us and to once more assert the link between personal pleasure and the needs of others — that is, the political dimension of desire:

'A sensual spirituality, then, is a political spirituality: it is about sharing the joys of the earth, of Creation. It is not - cannot be - about owning or accumulating power, immortality, control or rewards. It is sharing the pleasures of the earth by way of justice.'

> Matthew Fox — *Whee! We, Wee All the Way Home*

The Pernicious Dichotomies

We looked at polarities, or pairs of opposing views, in the early chapters of this work and in Chapter 4, mentioned Lawrence Cahoone's three 'pernicious dichotomies'. These are — subject and object, the split between the individual and the individual's relationships with others and the split between human culture and the natural realm.

The subject object split was examined in some detail as it is reflected so much in the way our culture views life. However, I want to draw out one further observation not given earlier in the text. This is to say that there is a more subtle interpretation of this dichotomy to be found. To understand it, we need to refer back first to what was said about existence and non-existence. We noted that our culture favours the idea of existence being brought forth out of a literal nothing, and contrasted this with existence emerging from chaos, or to put it another way, formlessness. We might say that the contrast is really between existence and emptiness rather than existence and non-existence. The universe then has emptied itself of form in order to become form. Our relationship with form therefore (that is, the subject object relation) is a more complex one than might first appear. So many of the authors quoted in this work talk about letting go or a setting aside of things — both material things and also our consistent habit of making ideas into images and abstract things which we then set up as 'objects' to be obtained. All of our quotes and indeed all of this work is inviting us to take away form and enter into formlessness. New form can then be created through us. It is not us who create form, as to believe this would make it into another compulsion - an ego striving to be something. Form and formlessness meet within us and we become form for others, that is, we become grace and all that flows from grace.

Cahoone's second dichotomy is addressed best I think by quotes from Simon Parke. In one he says simply, 'We hurt others by our unexamined pain.' And at the end of another quote is the simple sentence, 'We see outside us what is inside us.' Both of these simple sentences remind us firstly that much of the work of self-analysis is not about trying to discover or rediscover our ecstasy, but to understand our pain and our anger and our strange habitual responses. It is this blindness in ourselves that makes our relations with others difficult. Part of the problem, which refers back to our original two questions, is that things are stated from a purely individual point of view. It is *my* pleasure that I seek and it is the concern that the suffering of others gives *me*. The individual is essentially an abstraction. Ultimately, I am only myself in relationship with other selves. Pleasure, as I hope has been demonstrated, only makes sense within this broader context.

Cahoone's third dichotomy is about our dealing with the wider world of nature. Again, it might appear not to relate to our two questions — of desire and of need. However, Chapter 13 - The Soul Seeks Beauty First and Chapter 14 — Start with Awe, remind us of how intimately connected are our relationships with nature and our relationship with each other and with ourselves. Matthew Fox, amongst others, reminds us of our need for silence and for solitude and often these are sought within nature. Our relationship to the natural world is not one of standing outside it and trying to control it. Rather, wild nature resides right within us. Note how Simon Parke describes the essence of each of us as 'wonderful and wild'. When he speaks of our soul, it is of a '... cascading waterfall of experience, all power and fluidity, all change and force, all energy and life, a crashing vastness of possibility and engaged at every level of our physical and psychological well-being.' The conclusion is surely that our inner essence is linked with the wider world of nature just as much as with our own bodies.

Images and Ideals

We have noted the long-standing tendency to create perfect forms out of earthly virtues. It might be that these are projected onto a God or gods. Even without a religious belief though, even starting from mystery, there is a sense in which attributes might simply be projected and idealised. We use this as a means of seeking justification for moral absolutes, images of how we might wish the world to be.

Why not instead start with the reality of our own incarnation in the world — with 'Amo: volo ut sis.' (I love you: I will that you be.) Grace Jantzen, who we have quoted throughout this work, regards this phrase (from Hannah Arendt) as the ultimate ground for ethical action. Notice that 'will' here is used as a verb, and also that 'to be' is used in the predicative sense (and not to mean simply to exist). In using the phrase then, we are saying that we are creatively engaged to allow the other person to be themselves, to be all they can be, to flourish and live their lives fully. It is all action, in the truest sense of Agapé. It is mediated through us as a means of grace. But this is a grace already fully there in the world. For us to achieve this requires only for us to open a space within ourselves that will allow grace to operate. We look to deal with others as individuals rather than abstract collections of people. In knowing people by name, we respond to their face, we greet them as equals, we see their beauty, we have compassion with them in their vulnerability, because it is a vulnerability that we all share. We celebrate their humanity and in doing so, celebrate our own.

When we looked at meaning in Chapter 12, we noted that an over-arching meaning could be discerned from relationships but that this is nonetheless not a transcendent meaning. Likewise with beauty, whilst partly accepting beauty as an image or an ideal, we nonetheless saw actual encounters with beauty — nature, other people — as the inspiration for creating more beauty — for 'being pleasure'. The danger is always in 'commodifying' these values — making them something we seek to 'own' or 'appropriate' rather than something we live. What is it that makes grace and beauty different from say equality, justice or freedom? The difference is that grace and beauty *are given to us first*. They are the gifts from the universe, from which equality, compassion, justice, freedom and celebration all flow.

Loving something more than Death

This comes from our quote from Martin Luther King earlier in the work. So much of our culture is obsessed with death, but at the same time in denial of that obsession. The question, which links to the main questions of the work is, what is it that we should love more than death? We return to Grace Jantzen's contrast of natals over mortals. Simply stated then, it is the love of life over death. It might seem an obvious point, until we start to notice just how deeply ingrained the fascination with death runs in our culture. The work has traced this through a process. First, in seeing — noticing and observing — ourselves, others and nature. From there, the love for beauty, welcoming us and inspiring awe and gratitude. Exceptional beauty leads us in turn to see the beauty in ordinary things. We step outside ourselves. We seek fairness in our ordering of the world through equality. Equality is the starting point for compassion, justice and freedom. In this is our celebration and our joy. We create more beauty in the world, or rather grace works through us to create beauty. We are grace. We are the means of grace. In all this, we love life more than we love death.

What are we being asked to do?

It is very difficult for us to do nothing. We have an overwhelming drive to 'fix' things — to learn, or to educate, to solve problems by technical means, to devise bureaucracies in order to administer virtue and address the needs of the world. We are being told however that essentially, the kingdom of heaven is already here. Furthermore, there is not very much for us to do, except to step aside. It is for us only to open a space within and allow grace to flow. We might add here that despite the very real problems in the world, there is no need for us to strive, even although things may look desperate. It does not mean that we will not be deeply affected by circumstances, but the solution is always outside of us, even when we are the means of achieving it. The responsibility if you like is strangely lifted from us, even whilst in the human economy — a more limited world view — the burden of responsibility needs to remain. This quote from Hegel summarises this thought for us:

'The Good, the absolutely Good, is eternally accomplishing itself in the world; and the result is that it need not wait upon us but is *already in full actuality accomplished.*'

Also, reflected in our closing chapters, is the idea of making all these things personal. This means saying 'I am pleasure', 'I am love' and so on. Remember Ghandi's famous quote: 'Be the change you want to see in the world'. When we consider these statements in the first person present tense, how do we feel about them? As expressed in the final chapter, if I am not grace, there is no grace.

Viewed from eternity, a single human life can be said to be complete in itself. There is no future in which we will be different or any past that we need regret. We are at every moment all that we ever need to be. The same might be said of the world at large. On the broadest view, how can we ever say that it should be different to what it is?

The final Delusion

Doubt is a great leveller. Why not embrace doubt whole-heartedly? We have looked at twenty-one subjects where, it is contended, our culture is mistaken in its understanding of the issues raised. Our twenty-second and final delusion though, must surely be that all of the arguments made against culture are themselves delusional.

It would have been good to have had a narrative! It would have been good to present this work as a story about a person — ideally a person who lived the 'truth' of what is expressed herein! Remember the little quote at the start of Chapter 21 — 'If you want to communicate an idea, wrap it up in a person.' Religion is always going to be more popular than philosophy — and maybe that is the reason! Generally, it has stories, it has people. So, whilst the 'truths' expressed may be less clearly stated, the personal appeal is undeniable.

Well, in this book we have got souls and angels and grace — all terms borrowed from religion! Atheists may balk at my use of these terms. Meanwhile, the religious may well object to the notion that, for instance, our essence is already perfect, and there is no 'journey' to undertake, no need for 'salvation' or 'redemption' (at least in the traditional understanding of these terms).

The religious may also resent the suggestion that their particular faith is exclusively narrative. Refer back though to Grace Jantzen's idea that a 'natal's' expression will be 'performative' — '...they will tell stories', she says. I think we need new stories now. We need stories that will be understood as purely allegorical and not mixed up with history or with philosophy or theology. Alongside, we need stories of others that show grace at work. And perhaps most of all we need to weave our own encounters with the world into stories of who we are — of our adventure of essence in the world.

At the beginning of this work I suggested that anyone searching for answers should give up that search. This, as will hopefully be obvious, does not preclude an examined life. Any program however that purports to some kind of transcendent progress, to spiritual growth or to achieving enlightenment, heaven or nirvana is doomed to failure. We have to step aside from this. The only thing to do really is to create a space in our lives, a contemplative space of silence where we are simply observers of ourselves and our relations to others. A place to reflect on our encounters with nature and with other people and even our encounters with silence and mystery itself. A place where we take time to really see ourselves in a clear light and to see our circumstances and relationships. I suggest this is always a conflicted space. Made from mystery and deriving from darkness and chaos, we inevitably live a conflicted life day by day.

To quote again from the passage of Simon Parke's, given in Chapter 21:

'To receive truth, I need above all things to create something new inside me, a space not previously developed. I need to create a middle space, or in-between place — somewhere that is other than both my starting essence and my claustrophobic personality.'

That then becomes the foundation for action in the world. The space of which Parke talks lies beyond the boundaries that we have defined in this work. It is the opening for grace. But from there our work within the economies of human endeavour finds its true strength.

This is a process, not a once for all event. Conflict lies not just within ourselves. There is also conflict between us and the mystery that lies beyond us. Psychologist James Hillman suggests that our soul has her own purposes and merely uses us as her host — a bit like an extreme version of Philip Pullman's *His Dark Materials*. So, there will always be a conflict between essence and personality.

We finish now with a quote from Thomas Moore, which takes up this thought:

'We think that the ego is the dominant self, and we educate ourselves to have good ego boundaries, strong identity and self-esteem. But more enchanted philosophies recognise that we are made from the depths, from beyond consciousness. We are more original than we can imagine. *We are driven from a place beneath awareness,* and what drives us — it has been called angel, daimon, animus, duende — hurls us toward our identity and our place in time and space.

'W.B. Yeats saw that the daimon, the inner presence that is full of power and the ultimate source of our real creativity, is an antithetical self, an opposite, a spirit that is brought to a host precisely and utterly different from itself so that we often feel both *conflict and resource* in relation to the spirit that makes us *passionate*.'

> Thomas Moore — *Original Self* (my emphases).

So, it is a conflict that will never be resolved. But that's okay. No resolution is needed. Live with the doubt. Live with the mystery.